Quick Start to *Writing Workshop Success*

Easy and Effective Ways to Launch Your Writing Workshop—and Keep It Running Smoothly All Year Long!

Janiel Wagstaff

New York • Toronto • London • Auckland • Sydney
Mexico City • New Delhi • Hong Kong • Buenos Aires

DEDICATION

DEDICATION: For Max, who puts it all in perspective, and for Mom and Dad . . . still more patience, still more courage.

ACKNOWLEDGMENTS: Thanks again, Scholastic, especially editor extraordinaire Joanna Davis-Swing, Virginia Dooley, and Terry Cooper.

CONTACT INFO: For information on workshops and presentations or to contact Janiel, write to: janielwag@hotmail.com or phone (801) 546-6009.

Editor: Joanna Davis-Swing
Cover design: Jorge Jay Namerow
Interior design: LDL Designs
Cover photo: Jon Feingersh, Blend Images Photography
Interior photos: courtesy of the author
Copy editor: Chris Borris
Previously published as *20 Tricky Writing Problems–Solved!*

ISBN: 978-0-545-26717-5
Copyright © 2011 by Janiel Wagstaff
All rights reserved. Published by Scholastic Inc.
Printed in the U.S.A.
1 2 3 4 5 6 7 8 9 10   40   17 16 15 14 13 12 11

CONTENTS

INTRODUCTION

The more I work in schools, the more I see the need for a fresh look at writing. So many teachers feel angst when it comes to teaching the subject. They haven't had enough experience as writers themselves to feel confident in their teaching of writing. Though this is a natural reaction, the result is that students write sparingly, if at all. Many educators resort to assigning a few writing "projects" here and there—like reports or essays. Upper-elementary teachers scramble to do more writing because state and national tests now include essays based on prompts. The age of accountability, with heavy emphasis on raw scores, has added a new pressure for them. As a K–6 literacy coach in a Title I school, I hear upper-grade teachers complain that lower-grade teachers aren't doing enough writing, which results in students who come to them completely unprepared.

What's really happening here? For one, there's been such emphasis on reading research and practice that writing, once again, has been pushed to a back burner. Those of us who know writing well lament how shortsighted this is, since everything we do in writing translates to growth in reading, not to mention its host of other benefits. And, for some students, writing is pivotal in opening the door to reading success. Second, in addition to the indigestion some teachers feel about teaching writing, there's still a prevailing view that writing is being "done" if students publish some stories and reports throughout the school year. But, when our main goal is to produce lifelong, proficient writers, just as we strive to create lifelong readers, we see how small efforts and occasional dips into writing fail miserably to meet the mark.

In the end, a renewed emphasis on writing is needed. The research on writing workshop, work done by experts like Donald Graves, Lucy Calkins, Nancie Atwell, Ralph Fletcher and Joanne Portalupi, Regie Routman, Ruth Culham, and others, has brought more purposeful, explicit writing instruction into classrooms. Many students are happy participants in "writing communities," where writing is valued and enjoyed every day. How does this happen? Teachers run productive, balanced writing workshops and understand writing's place in every subject area throughout the entire day. Writing isn't an occasional event; it's always on the menu.

The purpose of this book, then, is twofold: First, just like the National Commission on Writing (2003), I hope to push writing forward again, into its proper place, equal in weight to reading. Our goals for writers should mirror our ambitious goals for readers. Second, I'd like to provide simple strategies that work for teaching writing in classrooms from grade 2 on up—doable strategies even novice teachers can put in place with ease. These include best practices for implementing and maintaining a balanced writing workshop

AND using writing as a tool for learning across the curriculum. The book is short, to the point, and aimed at providing a "Quick Start to Writing Workshop Success." I hope more teachers will embrace these techniques and confidently take on the challenge of writing with students. If they do, if you do, you will be hooked on the power and value of writing!

Putting It in Perspective

One of my favorite quotes on the power of putting writing into proper perspective:

"Above all, as students and young adults begin a lifetime of learning, they will find that writing is liberating, satisfying, even joyful. Writing is not simply a way for students to demonstrate what they know. It is a way to help them understand what they know. At its best, writing is learning . . . . As a nation, we can barely begin to imagine how powerful K–16 education might be if writing were put into its proper focus. Facility with writing opens students up to the pleasure of exercising their minds in ways that drilling on facts, details, and information never will. More than a way of knowing, writing is an act of discovery."

—*The National Commission on Writing (2003, pp. 13–14)*

Part I: Quick Start Guide

CHAPTER 1:

Quick Start Tips

First: Schedule It and Stick to It!

How do you go about getting a quick start to writing success? First and foremost, you put writing in its proper perspective. It is essential to students' success in school and life. Successful writing teachers set aside a sustained period of time for writing every day and they take advantage of what I call "quick bursts" of writing across the curriculum throughout the day. Their schedules are as jam-packed as the next teacher's, but they realize the potential writing has for teaching a plethora of skills and they adjust accordingly. Anything of questionable value comes out of their day, while the teaching of conventions, mechanics, spelling, and grammar is integrated into everyday writing. They have a "no excuses" attitude and wouldn't dream of leaving writing out of their schedules. Writing never suffers when another new curriculum initiative comes down the pike. Rather, the best teachers think, "How can my students process this new material through writing?" Writing can bolster all learning, and be a source of joy as well.

Wow! That sounds like a tall order, right? I'll make you this promise: If you start writing every day with your students, stick with it (you don't give up when you have a bad day AND you don't allow other things to push writing out), and implement even a few ideas in this book, you will be sold 100 percent. You'll see how your students love the process, grow as thinkers, and develop solid skills in mechanics and spelling. And you'll be on your way to becoming a die-hard, skillful teacher of writing!

Second: Get Rid of Self-Doubt— You CAN Successfully Teach Writing!

I often begin teacher workshops on writing with a few questions. "How many of you consider yourselves readers?" Everyone in the crowd raises their hand. Then I ask, "Now, how many of you consider yourselves writers?" Unvaryingly, less than ten percent, and usually only about five percent, raise their hands. Why is this? Most of us consider ourselves proficient readers. We read a lot throughout the day, we enjoy reading, we choose to read, and we read with ease. But most of us do not consider ourselves proficient writers. We may write quite a bit throughout the day (often without even realizing it), but we don't choose to write for recreation and we don't write with ease. Most of us write formally only when we are required to do so. Naturally, our own sense of self-efficacy spills over into our teaching. We're comfortable teaching reading, but not writing.

Here's a Quick Start tip: GET RID OF THE DOUBT! You CAN successfully teach writing! Like anything else, your skills in this area will develop with practice. The practice doesn't have to be painful . . . it can even be fun! As I converse with teachers about writing, I hear how unsettled they are about teaching it. They're full of questions and they worry they're not going to "do it right." The key is not to expect perfection. Don't think you should know it all right out of the chute (we never know it all, anyway). Acknowledge you may be out of your comfort zone but embrace the opportunity to learn alongside students. This might begin with something as simple as asking students to jot down their thoughts about what happened in the classroom—as you do the same. Allow them to share, discuss what they wrote, and see what happens.

Consider the flip side. If you don't make time for writing, you can be absolutely certain your skills as a teacher of writing won't improve. If you don't make time for writing, you can be equally certain your students' skills won't improve. In the end, do you really have a choice? This book will show you easy ways to dive into the process with success, and again, I can promise you this: Once you see how students respond, you won't go back.

Third: Think Balance— A Lot of Writing Should Be Informal

I began my journey into teaching writing more than 20 years ago after hearing a junior-high English teacher talk about writing workshop. I was convinced I wasn't doing enough writing with my students and that I could teach language arts objectives through writing rather than separate from writing. I also felt I could get my students fired up and motivated to write a lot by using a workshop approach. There were many things I did well that first year and many things I did not understand.

Though I was devoting daily time to writing and following a workshop routine, empowering choice and allowing students to work through the process at their own pace, I erred in having them create final, published products for almost everything they'd written. I now understand writing should be treated just like reading. I don't require my students to do something formal with everything they read. That would be ridiculous! If I did, it would take tons of time, which, in turn, would diminish other opportunities to read. When I think about it, I realize we read in a variety of ways—sometimes for a sustained period, sometimes for just a few minutes at a time—for a variety of purposes, throughout the day. We're learning to read while using reading as a learning tool. The same should be true for writing. We need to write all day long, sometimes for sustained periods and sometimes for just a few minutes at a time. We need to write for a variety of purposes. We need to use writing as a thinking tool throughout the entire day—yes, while we're learning to write. And we definitely need to engage in heaps of writing that is informal, like taking a few moments to quickly jot, respond, question, list, or brainstorm without any intent to move further through the steps of the writing process or to publish. I'll show you how this plays out throughout the book.

Another point of balance is to realize, as with reading, we do not need to monitor everything children write. Readers are given many opportunities to read throughout the day—some with teacher guidance, some without. Learners make all kinds of mistakes when they are learning to read, yet we understand the amount of reading they do—the sheer volume and practice garnered—are vital to their growth. We don't feel the need to be there, right beside them, correcting all of their mistakes. Why do we feel the need to do this to our writers? Many teachers don't write much with students because they say they don't have time to respond to and correct it all. What if we don't have to respond to and correct it all? No one would say this about reading . . . and no one should say this about writing. The truth is, we need to provide a variety of writing experiences, some formal, some informal, some with feedback and guidance, some without, some shared, some independent, just as we do with reading. It's that simple . . . and realizing this can be very liberating. It may help you look at writing in a whole new way!

One more thing: Writing need not be characterized as strictly formal (worked through the process) or informal (not worked through the process). Instead, think of the gradations in between. For example, if you give an assignment, you might tell students they'll be meeting with a peer group to share their content and check two areas you've been focusing on in instruction: use of capitals and the spelling of high-frequency, irregular words (or "no-excuses words" [Sitton, 1999]). In this case, there are some checks and balances, but you're not expecting the work to go through all the steps to formal publishing (see Circling Skills We Know, page 63).

Inside My Writing Classroom: A Brief Overview

I have a "writing mind-set" in my classroom. That means I'm always thinking about how writing fits into what we're learning and how we can learn through writing. If I give my students multiple opportunities to stop, think, and jot, even for two or three minutes, they'll process content more deeply than if they don't write. Another benefit is they'll acclimate quickly to facing a blank page, since it's a frequent part of our

Learning Through Writing

I share with students this quote from E. B. White to help them understand how we use writing as a tool for learning: "How do I know what I think until I see what I write?" In essence, writing takes concentrated precision not achieved in oral language. We clarify our thoughts by putting them on paper, then examine them in a highly focused manner, discovering questions, even gaps, in our knowledge. Written language can undergo refining, rehearsal, revision—thus enabling us to achieve a much more complete understanding of our own thinking and learning. For example, when I write books for teachers, I write to clarify my practice, look at it closely, understand it more thoroughly, and remember it vividly. Every time I write about teaching, I learn more about the hows and the whys of my practice. That's learning *through* writing. Liken this to an idea we all know well: Students learn more when they actually teach others what they've learned. Why? When we teach, we rehearse in our minds what will be said, how something will be demonstrated, what examples we might use, and so on. As we plan this, we discover subtleties in our understandings we didn't know existed. It is the same with writing.

daily routine. Additionally, of course, their writing skills will improve with the extra practice they're getting during these events.

For example, if I want to know what students believe they've learned from surveying their peers on the playground, I ask them to think about it and jot a few words or phrases in their "Think Pad." This gives them time to organize their thoughts and apply writing skills. Then, we briefly share. Students see their writing has purpose, their ideas are respected, and our discussions are always richer when preceded by writing. Often, students add ideas to their Think Pad during sharing.

These "quick bursts of writing" happen all day long, across the curriculum. I've included several examples in this book. My students don't groan when I ask them to write. It's simply part of everything we do—again, just like reading. You may ask, What about the students who have limited writing/spelling skills? What are they supposed to do? They write, just like the rest of us. How? The best they can. And, with excellent, targeted instruction that supports their development, their skills grow exponentially.

The other key component of my writing classroom is daily writing workshop. We use a simple, three-part format.

Think Pads

Every year, stores have blowout back-to-school sales. I buy enough ten-cent, 90-page spiral notebooks for everyone to keep in their desks—plus extras for students who fill up their first Think Pad. We write in them, and we diagram, chart, and draw right over the lines.

- We start with a **ten-minute mini-lesson** during which we practice routines and procedures and explore author's craft, the writing process, strategies, conventions, and genres. To demonstrate writing points, I often use children's books, samples of students' writing on the overhead or document camera, or my own writing as a model. Many of the lessons, strategies, and routines discussed in this book are introduced and reinforced during this mini-lesson time.

- Next, we have a **30-minute writing time** during which everybody writes and I confer with students (see explanation below). We call this Open Writing Time (see box, right).

- We close with a **ten-minute sharing time**, including time for everyone to share with a partner as well as opportunities for whole-class sharing through the Author's Chair (see Managing Sharing Time, page 22).

I introduce the format on the first day of school by saying, "We are all writers. We all have things to say and stories to tell. In our class, we'll write every day. We'll start by coming together for a short lesson where we'll talk about what writers do. Then, everyone will have time to write and we'll close our workshop by sharing our writing. This is the plan we'll follow every day—we'll meet, talk, write, and share—so you can count on this time and plan ahead."

During the 30-minute writing time, students take out their Think Pads or writing folders, look over what they have, and continue to work. They may be engaged in the following activities.

Building Stamina With Open Writing

We begin the year with only about ten minutes of Open Writing Time. As students learn how to use the time and manage themselves, the time increases and builds up to 30 minutes (or more). Again, I draw a parallel to reading here. When I begin guided reading groups, I keep them short as students learn how to use their independent reading time. This ensures success for everyone and also gives a sense of urgency—since the time is short, they learn to get right to work!

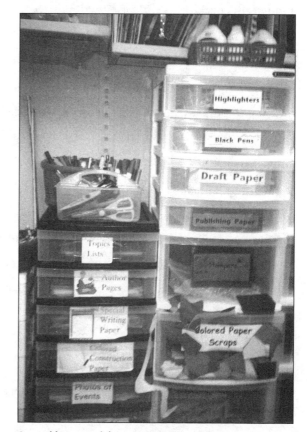

Our writing materials center

Prewriting: Students plan for their writing through reading sources, brainstorming, talking, sketching, or rereading writing they've already done. They may also be generating topics and adding to their Running Topics List (see page 20).

Drafting: Students write independently on a topic of their choice in a variety of genres (poems, letters, stories, informational articles, etc.) or work on an assigned piece. They are always encouraged to do their best work, using the writing conventions they know and their best spelling.

Revising: Students reread what they've already written and make appropriate changes to the content. This mainly occurs simultaneously as students draft. They are taught to stop frequently and reread, checking to see if their writing says what they want it to say and sounds its best (see Modeled Writing, Chapter 4).

Special library section: Books we've authored

Editing: Students go back through their writing to fix and circle their use of proper conventions, mechanics, and spelling (see Circling Skills We Know, page 63). This is not required with every piece, but is done on pieces going to publishing.

Publishing: Students formally present chosen pieces of writing in a finished format. This may mean producing a book by rewriting (or typing) a draft once it's been reviewed and binding it into a folder, adding a cover and illustrations; typing a poem in bold lettering and posting it on a classroom wall; rewriting a letter on stationery and mailing it; or reading a piece to an audience in another classroom.

During the 30-minute writing time, the teacher either confers—meeting with individual students to respond to their content, provide assistance, and/or help with revision and editing—or calls groups together to work on a particular writing issue.

A Note on Collaboration

Any of these steps may involve work with a peer or group. Students are encouraged to collaborate when they need response or help. The more a piece or idea is spoken aloud, the more the piece (or part of the composition) or idea can be shaped and sharpened. I liken reading and rereading aloud to a painter stepping back to examine her latest strokes—it's just part of the ongoing process.

I wait to begin conferring with students for several weeks into the workshop so I can circulate throughout the room during writing time. This allows me to give immediate encouragement, help, and feedback to all writers and reinforce routines.

Students write in their Think Pads and they also have two-pocket folders to manage their works in progress. If they choose to publish a letter, for example, the loose piece of stationery is kept in the folder until work is finished and the letter is mailed or given to its recipient.

I emphasize that writing is precious—it represents the students' hearts and minds. Therefore, we never throw any writing away. Instead, we date everything. This is critical since we must be able to evaluate our own writing progress and show it to parents and administrators. If a student is working on a piece that is not bound in her notebook and she decides not to continue, she turns it in and I file it. Later, if she changes her mind, I can retrieve it and work can resume. Writers never know when they may want to refer back to an idea they've written down. The "no throw away" policy ensures accountability, honors process, and establishes the great worth of our writing efforts.

The decisions I make about running the workshop and responding to students are grounded in a simple philosophy: *Treat students like real writers and they will view themselves as and behave like real writers.* Giving them choice, respect, and serious-minded instruction while showing them the joys of writing works wonders.

Setting Short-Term Goals

We're all anxious to teach—after all, there always seems to be so much to cover! But, we must use caution when starting out with our writers. The following section covers how critically important the right kinds of short-term goals are for student success.

SETTING THE TONE, GETTING THEM WRITING

Starting students out on the right writing foot is critical. As Ralph Fletcher and JoAnn Portalupi (2001) note, teachers must keep a few short-term goals in mind before getting ahead of themselves worrying about the long-term ones. First, we must get students to love and feel safe about writing. Again, think about reading. We want students to love reading and choose to read. So, we plan our beginnings carefully, choosing to read aloud fun, exciting books while surrounding students with things they CAN read. We work hard to foster motivation and success. BINGO! The same must happen with writing.

Here's an example of failing to put short-term goals first. In my school district, a high-stakes writing assessment happens in fifth grade. In early spring, our fifth graders complete a persuasive essay based on a prompt that is then analytically scored on a four-point scale. Feeling the pressure, teachers often begin the year thinking of how they want students to perform on that assessment, so they start right off assigning persuasive pieces, requiring students to work through the entire writing process to publish. Ouch! This is a painful place to start and it sets a very harsh writing tone for the school year. Instead, we want to begin by actively building students' self-esteem as writers, while giving them time to get excited about writing in a nonthreatening environment.

How is this accomplished? What we assign and engage students in must have a "can-do" feel. I begin by sharing lots of examples of writing done by students from years past. As I share samples (on the overhead or with the document camera), I show great enthusiasm and respect for *what* was written (not necessarily *how* it was written). I point out what is good (even if it's one word or phrase, or one idea). Right away, students notice the writing isn't "perfect," yet it is fun, worthwhile, and honored. This little trick goes a long way toward letting them know they can be successful.

I also share examples of commercially published writing that has a "doable" feel. For example, one of my favorites is *Little Dog Poems* by Kristine O'Connell George (1999). The voice is a young girl writing simple poems (some consisting of just five words) about an everyday thing she loves: her dog. It's delightful. Students see that just a few words on a page can be entertaining and have an impact.

Ish and *The Dot* (2004, 2003—thanks, Peter Reynolds!) are two books I read aloud at the beginning of every year. They help me set the tone for a safe writing environment and model the way I will respond and students will be expected to respond to one another's writing. In *Ish*, Ramon draws and draws, anytime, anywhere (I make the analogy that we will "write and write, anytime, anywhere"), until his older brother makes fun of one of his drawings. The negative response "haunts" Ramon and he stops drawing. But, later, his younger sister sees him doodling and runs away with the drawing. When Ramon chases her into her room, he sees her walls are covered with drawings he has crumpled up and thrown away because they weren't perfect. Her positive response, pointing out how one of his drawings looks "vase-ish," inspires Ramon to begin drawing again, freely and creatively. His ish-drawings inspire ish-writings! The points I drive home with *Ish* include: Writing doesn't have to be perfect to be enjoyable and valuable; taking risks is a good thing; and the response we give one another heavily impacts how we feel about ourselves as writers and what we accomplish as writers. Our mantra becomes: Our community of writers WILL be positive and we'll always seek to inspire more writing from one another. In *The Dot*, Vashti thinks she can't draw, so she doesn't. Her art teacher responds to a dot she angrily jabs on a paper by . . . framing it and hanging it on the wall! This motivates Vashti to draw and paint even better dots. Ultimately, her dots end up in the school art show and Vashti reassures another wayward artist he can do it, too. Oh, the power of positive response! Both books are invaluable.

As we begin the year, then, students write, share, and "publish" pieces to the best of their abilities (no revision or editing is required). The writings are often short and full of errors. I am undaunted by this. I see the same pattern year after year, no matter the grade level (that is, unless I'm working at a school where writing is truly valued, well taught, and part of children's everyday experience). My goal is first and foremost to simply get students writing, increase their ease and fluency, and show them that their voices are valued. Naturally, their initial writings also provide great baseline data and show me a lot about what concepts, skills, and strategies need to be taught.

DAY ONE

What does the first day of school look like, then? After an entertaining read-aloud about the challenges of the first day of school (something everyone can relate to), I pass out the Think Pads, telling the class we'll use them to jot down our thoughts several times a day. We open to the first page, date it, and write one word—just one word—about how we are feeling starting school. Naturally, I invite students to write more if they wish. I model, writing in my own Think Pad. After just a minute or so, I ask if anyone would like to share. Student volunteers read their one word (or more) and I comment—I talk with them (just as if we were casually talking), asking questions and relating to what they've written, and invite others to do so, as well. This simple exercise launches our journey into thinking, jotting down thoughts, discussing, elaborating, and honoring one another's voices across the curriculum every day.

Later in the morning, I open our writing workshop for the year by explaining the three parts of the workshop and celebrating a few previous students' pieces ("Look what you might write!"). Then, I share examples of the "talk" I've heard throughout the morning and how that talk might lead to writing. I might say something like:

I've been listening and making notes about some of the things you've been talking about this morning. The things we talk about are things we care about, and often they can turn into things we write about. For example, I heard Shayna say some of her friends were arguing at the bus stop about the school's dress code. Shayna might write about that, simply jotting down what she heard so she can further think it through or writing a letter to the principal to get clarification about the dress code so she can pass that information along to her friends. I overheard Jafrad commenting about riding to school on his scooter this morning. Apparently, he has a new scooter and is just learning to ride. How's that going, Jafrad? [pause for student to comment] *He can use his writing time to write about that. Okay, we'd better get writing! As we begin this process, our Open Writing Time will be short. So use it well!*

Short-Term Goals

- Get students writing (in quick bursts and in workshop)
- Celebrate students' writing
- Set up a safe environment
- Establish the three parts of the workshop
- Begin Running Topics List
- Teach and practice procedures for sharing

With that, I circulate and celebrate, giving immediate positive feedback and help. Much encouragement is needed during the early days, so I walk around and comment aloud for all to hear. "I see Ciera has chosen to write about her dog. This will make a great topic since it's close to her heart and something she knows a lot about." "Oh! Jenson is writing a letter. Good for him! Writers love to try different forms of writing." "Look here! Diego has crossed out a whole sentence. He's changing something in his writing. Good writers know they can make changes and experiment with their words and ideas." (See Building Motivation by Celebrating Students' Writing, page 17, for more.)

I circulate for the entire ten-minute writing time, then say, "That's all the time we'll have for writing workshop today, but you'll have more time tomorrow. Additionally, you can *always* work on your writing—anytime you have extra time in class. During our time today, you may have written something you really like, or you may not feel so great about what you wrote. Either way, that's okay. Would anyone like to share?" After a few students share, and I model giving thoughtful responses, we close the workshop for the day.

Throughout the rest of the day, I make sure to work in at least two more quick jotting times in our Think Pads. I want students to get the idea we'll be working in these pads a lot. And, like the example of writing just one word above, I want them to feel they can *do* the writing and their thoughts and ideas will be appreciated. I keep it short and simple. For example, during math, after completing some data gathering on students' favorite outdoor activities, I ask them to jot down a few words, phrases, or sentences about what they observe or conclude when they look at the data. We share and talk about our thoughts for three or four minutes.

WEEK ONE

Each day of the first week follows the same pattern: three or four Quick Jots (see page 29) in Think Pads followed by brief talk (these are spread throughout the day) and a shortened writing workshop. My initial goals include getting students writing (in quick bursts AND in workshop), celebrating their efforts, setting up a safe environment, and establishing the three routine parts of the workshop. We also start our Running Topics List (see page 20) and work on procedures for sharing. The first few weeks look much the same, with continued emphasis on short-term goals.

If there are students who don't write during these opportunities throughout the first week, I make a point to meet with them. I reassure them, "I'll bet you have a lot of great ideas. We can't wait to hear what you have to say. Don't worry if you've been feeling nervous. The writing will come." How do I make good on that promise? By continuing to make writing doable (with short, easy assignments and choice), by encouraging and celebrating efforts, and, ultimately, when my long-term goals kick in, through that "serious-minded instruction" I mentioned earlier. This includes the explicit teaching strugglers need, which you'll see in Part II. For now, let's turn our attention to the essential routines and procedures that will help make your workshop a success right from the start.

CHAPTER 2

Essentials for Quick Success

Next, we continue to focus on developing and supporting our short-term goals. These essentials for quick success will help you with engagement, management, topic generation, and sharing and responding.

Building Motivation by Celebrating Students' Writing

I've already mentioned the power of celebrating students' writing, but I'd like to cover this topic more completely since it is so critical to start the year and it is a mainstay throughout the year. You can celebrate writing by making positive remarks aloud as you circulate, modeling positive response during sharing times, and showing student samples on the overhead or with the document camera during mini-lessons. (Naturally, the effect is greater when students can *see* the samples.)

If you're a novice writing teacher, how can you celebrate your students' writing? Easily. During your first Quick Jot (see page 29), your first Quick Write (see page 38), or your first workshop, someone will write something that catches your attention. It may be the content or the unique voice but, if you look, you will find it—from Day 1. It's as easy as: "I asked you to jot down one word about how you were

Content Over Mechanics

Here's an important point: Please, please focus on the content—not the mechanics. It never fails, when I share this strategy in teacher workshops, the first things participants want to celebrate in great writing samples are things like "She used a capital in the proper place!" or "He spelled a lot of words correctly!" Remember your short-term goals. You can focus on mechanics later; first help students see you're interested in their ideas.

feeling starting school. Look here! Sandra did exactly that . . . and a whole lot more!" Sandra's sample is read aloud while projected with the document camera. Your comments might include how she successfully wrote on the topic assigned and how you can relate to what she's written. That's it! You're on your way.

One note of caution: I NEVER use a student's piece as a negative example. Though non-examples are certainly beneficial in helping students clarify concepts, using a *current* student's writing as such undermines motivation, self-efficacy, and the safe writing climate. Rather, when sharing a non-example, I use samples I purposely create (see Peer Revision Activities, page 55) or samples from previous students with all identifying information removed.

To emphasize the value and importance of celebrating students' writing, let me share this: It is the *first* strategy I demonstrate to teacher audiences whenever I'm speaking about writing. It's so quick and easy, and it can have an enormous impact on motivation and engagement. I stress the use of three types of examples:

1.   Samples that make writing seem "doable" to students

2.   Samples that show a variety of writing abilities, so students know their attempts will be accepted

3.   Later, samples that can be used to make teaching points

As you get going, remember the positive use of your current students' examples carries more weight than any other writing you may use as models.

Let's look at a few. Say it is your first week of school and you show these samples to the class using the document camera. What might you celebrate? Take a few minutes and consider each one. Be sure to focus on the content and be positive. Your main goal is to make your students comfortable and get them writing.

This fourth grader wrote: "My favorite hobby is getting pulled behind a bike on a skateboard. It helps you overcome your fear of speed. I was scared to go fast, but now I'm not. Next when you're going fast you let go of the rope. It's fun riding in puddles. Third, I once tried standing up. It was hard. So I tried sitting down. It was easy. Last, I love the wind when it blows in my face." I'd celebrate his unusual hobby; experimentation with transitions; and use of several specific examples from his experience, such as "I once tried standing up. It was hard. So, I tried sitting down. It was easy." (Interesting compare and contrast statements!) His examples expand the reader's understanding of why being pulled behind a skateboard is his favorite hobby.

I'd celebrate this student's authentic voice; use of emphasis (words in all capitals); word choice; attention to a small event in his life and use of that little happening for a writing topic; and effort in taking his writing through to publishing.

> ## Wasabi Peas
> by Riley
>
> My Mom says, "Mmmmmmmm,"
> My Dad says, "Mmmmmmmm,"
> but I say, "YUCK!"
> "YUCK!" "YUCK!"
> "YUCK!" "YUCK!"
> "YUCK!" "YUCK!"
> I HATE THEM!
> They love them!
> They're crazy!

HINTS FOR SUCCESS

1. If you're unsure what to celebrate, you might focus on these simple ideas, especially to begin the year.

    ✦ **Topic Choice:** If it was assigned, did the student stick to the topic? If it was not assigned, where did the topic come from? Life experiences? Books or other reading materials? Imagination? The Running Topics List?

    ✦ **Risk Taking:** Showcase examples that take risks in topic selection, or creativity with voice, ideas, sketching/drawing/presentation, or even in spelling a particularly powerful but difficult word.

    ✦ **Production:** Celebrate prolific writers. For example, say, "Wow! Look at what Sammi wrote during our first Open Writing Time. She must have had a lot to say and she sure used her time well!"

    ✦ **Using the Traits:** Let the 6+1 Traits of Writing model guide you (see Culham, 2003, for more information). Celebrate students' ideas, voice, word choice, sentence fluency, organization, or presentation (wait to celebrate conventions until later).

    ✦ For more ideas, see those listed under Ongoing Teacher Modeling of Responding Skills, page 25.

2. Show a piece and ask the writer to tell you and the class about it. Demonstrating your interest in her ideas will go a long way.

3. Don't wait for a "perfect piece" to celebrate . . . you may be waiting a very long time! Find a choice word, an innovative sentence, one paragraph or an idea—a strong part. Highlight that portion! Don't forget to tame your critical teacher lens—wait until you move into long-term goals.

Making Sure Everyone Is Ready to Write

The first few minutes of each day's workshop are important, especially in the beginning weeks of the school year. Here's a management technique designed to ensure a productive start. After my mini-lesson, I simply ask, "Who's ready to write?" Hands shoot up, and if there's time, I ask a few writers to tell us what they'll be working on. Then, those who are ready go back to their seats take out their Think Pads or grab a piece of writing paper, date the page, and write. Those who are hesitant stay together in our meeting place and I ask questions like "What's going on in your life that you might write about?" or "Did we read anything today that gave you an idea for writing?" or "Is anyone stuck with something in particular?" We talk a bit more, which stimulates thinking, and students trickle back to their seats ready to write. If some are particularly stubborn about starting their writing, I might say, "I need to be available to all our writers. Go back to your seat and put your pencil to the page. See what happens. If you remain stuck, you might get up and walk around to look at what others are doing. This may get you going." As you'd expect, I make a point of quickly checking in with these writers as I circulate.

Finding Something to Write About: The Running Topics List

In order for students to write, they have to have something to write about. With the quick bursts of writing I've mentioned, the content we're studying drives the writing (you'll see this later). What about during the workshop time? Many teachers find it difficult to get students into the habit of continuously generating their own topics. They ask, "How do your students know what to write about? Do you always just assign them topics?" Balance is key. In the real world, writers sometimes complete assignments; other times, they write on topics they've developed themselves. Our student writers should experience the same. So, when we're not assigning a topic, how do students come up with their own? And how do we help them do this across a variety of genres?

A Running Topics List on the side of your board is one easy answer. It allows you to model topic generation throughout the day and demonstrate that writers are always looking and listening for writing ideas. It further enables you to show how topics can come up anytime, anywhere. Opportunities to stop and add to the list abound in the daily workings of any classroom. Like the students, you must develop a mind-set for writing—the habit of listening and watching to catch writing topics. When you hear a student share something that may lead to writing, take a moment and jot a note on the Running Topics List. You might think aloud, "I heard Chad say his family moved over the summer. Imagine his feelings and the new challenges this presents. Many ideas for writing may come out of this event. I'd better take a moment right now to jot a note on our Running Topics List before this idea is forgotten." As you talk, walk to the board and write something like "Chad: moving." If time permits, you may also discuss how this could lead to a story, poem, or letter and add a notation like "poem about feelings." This example only pertains to one student, but the act of stopping, commenting on the possibility for writing, and jotting it down teaches important topic-generation habits. As I use the Running Topics List in my classroom, I make sure to balance the ideas

I note; some are directed toward individuals, others toward everyone. Additionally, I'm careful the examples represent multiple genres.

Here's another example: During our morning reading share time, Lanae shares a few lines from the book *Junie B. Jones Is a Beauty Shop Guy* (Park, 1998). I comment, "So, Junie B. wants to be a beautician? What a great idea for writing! Any of us could write our own piece about what we want to be when we grow up. This might lead to a poem or story, or you might even do some research into the job you may want to have. Often, the things we read give us ideas to write about, and this Junie B. book is another example of that! I better take a second and jot it down. Later, during Writing Workshop, you may want to start a piece on one of these ideas."

One year, my students voted to get a newt as a class pet. We spent a lot of time reading and observing to find out all we could about our new friend. One afternoon, while Tamera was watching the newt swim, she said, "I see the colors of the rainbow on his skin. A rainbow of newt!" I capitalized on this, saying, "How wonderful! That would make an interesting subject for a poem, and perhaps 'Rainbow of Newt' could be the title! Tamera, take a moment and add the idea of newt poetry to our list. Class, think of all the possibilities for writing about the newt. We've learned many unique facts about newts and salamanders. You could research other questions you have and write an informational piece. That would make a useful addition to our classroom newspaper. We could inform parents of facts about our pet! Who can think of other ideas?" During our brief discussion, several students added ideas to the board.

As you can imagine, a robust list of relevant topic ideas is created in no time. More important, though, students become adept at consistently noticing writing opportunities. I remind them to jot any ideas they like on their *own* lists as we begin our writing workshop. An easy way

WWS
School dress code
Jafrad: scooter
Chad—moving:
    poem about feelings
Grown-up jobs
Our newt

A class Running Topics List in Progress

Tips:

- Make additions to the list *throughout* the day, not just during language arts time. Be sure to include ideas across multiple content areas, genres, and purposes.
- Celebrate when students write about something from the list. As you circulate around the room, take note of those who've recorded ideas from the board on their own lists. Show examples on the document camera to encourage all students to use the Running Topics List as a resource.
- Use an idea listed as a springboard for your own Modeled Writing project (see page 45).

to manage this is to have them start their own Running Topics Lists on the last page of their Think Pads and work backwards in their notebooks as they add to their list. As we run out of space on our board, I remind students I'll erase the class list at the end of the day, so they need to record any ideas they like before the ideas are gone. I begin this process on the very first day of school and continue it all year. Obviously, the ability to generate topics is fundamental to quick success, but overall, my hope is to instill a lifelong writing habit.

Managing Sharing Time

Honoring students' voices is crucial to setting and maintaining a motivating writing climate, so it's important to encourage sharing and responding from day one. How is that accomplished? We spend just three to four minutes sharing after each quick burst of writing. At these times, I simply ask for volunteers to read from their Think Pads and I model response, which includes paraphrasing, questioning, and relating to deepen our discussion. Some teachers keep this process fair by "pulling sticks." If at any time I have too many volunteers, I call on students by their day of the week (see explanation in "Author's Chair," below). Another strategy is to complete the three to four minutes of responding with the class, then allow anyone who still wants to share to turn to their neighbor and do so.

Since writing workshop involves a longer period of sustained writing time than the quick bursts do, I acknowledge students' need for collaboration *as* they write. There is always a low buzz as students help one another solve problems or they quietly share and respond during Open Writing Time. Depending on one another adds a cooperative, comfortable quality to our workshop. Given this openness, you'd think sharing would take care of itself. Yet, there is something about the formal sharing time *after* writing that presents a challenge. Year after year, I've dealt with the problem of too many students wanting to share in our Author's Chair (that special place, where one has everyone's undivided attention). I remind students we have a schedule

Pulling Sticks

Pulling Sticks is a popular management strategy used to equalize turns. Each student's name is written on a popsicle stick and placed in a can. When volunteers are needed, the teacher pulls a stick from the can and offers that student the choice of participating. Once his/her turn is used, the stick is placed in a second can. When the first can is empty, all students have had a turn and the process begins again.

Author's Chair

I schedule students' Author's Chair time by the days of the week (Cunningham, 1995). The first five students on my class list share on Mondays, the next five or six share on Tuesdays, and so on through Friday.

by days of the week to keep things fair, and that during workshop time, they can always ask another writer for response. Still, without special *after*-writing share time, there's usually a slew of extra requests for the Author's Chair: "Ms. Wag, pleeeease! I need to share today. It's not my assigned day, but I wrote something soooo good. I know our writers will want to hear it!"

I solve this problem by closing the writing portion of our workshop with an Everybody Share Time preceding Author's Chair. During this two- or three-minute period, students find a partner and read a bit of their writing, one at a time, to each other. This simple trick seems to satisfy the daily need for routine after-writing share time. Students know if they do not move quickly, the time will be gone. They may choose to skip their Everybody Share Time for the day and continue writing. But once those few minutes are up, they are up! So when students complain they did not get to share, I say, "Everyone has time to share every day during Everybody Share Time. How did you use your sharing time today?"

I do not extend this short sharing time. I truly keep it to two or three minutes. Students learn to work within these constraints. Additionally, by keeping the time consistently limited, we always have plenty of time for Author's Chair.

POTENTIAL PITFALL

Teachers sometimes leave out sharing time because schedules are so packed. This is a huge mistake! It's better to cut the writing time a bit shorter and keep the sharing time. Why? First, the talk feeds the writing. When students share, their peers get ideas about what to write and how to write. We are all models for one another. It builds community and competence. Second, sharing lends purpose to writing. Imagine writing every day and simply stuffing your work in a drawer. What purpose does that serve? Over time, you'd lose motivation. This is the last thing we want for our students. Giving one's writing a voice through sharing is vital to motivation.

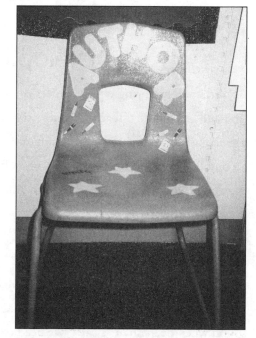

MANAGING THE AUTHOR'S CHAIR

My Author's Chair has hosted hundreds of writers over the years. I've learned it's useful to have a few simple rules to keep things running smoothly. First, when their day of the week comes up, writers know they have the option to share or pass. If they choose to share, their job is to be prepared. Most students use their Everybody Share Time or even some of their writing time to get ready.

Our Author's Chair

Students may share *anything* they are working on. This may be a finished piece, a piece in process, a title, an illustration, or an idea. But the rule is they can only share that particular thing *once*. I found this rule to be especially important in the primary grades because students would tend to come forward and share the same story over and over. True, they had worked on the piece for a whole week before their time came up again, but starting from the beginning and reading something over and over is not engaging. The audience loses interest.

This rule is not meant to discourage writers. Rather, it is meant to keep our sharing on track and interesting for everyone. Also, it sets a standard for making writing progress in order to have the *privilege* of sharing. Students realize if they don't use their writing time well, they'll have nothing new to share. Since they covet their time in the Author's Chair, this is an extra motivator.

One caveat: When students write pieces that take several sessions to complete, they *can* share what's *new*. In this case, they take a few seconds for an introduction, but what is shared is different from before. Balta, a fourth grader, recently told the class, "You know I've been working on a letter to the president about the oil spill. I've made some changes and added to the closing and I want to hear what you think."

Lastly, students know they have only a few precious minutes in the Author's Chair. Naturally, they often write pieces that are much too lengthy to share in a few short minutes. In these cases, students are allowed to share up to two pages. They may give us a brief synopsis beforehand, but what is actually read is limited. It's not a perfect solution, but it works. Again, students always have the option of seeking response during our Open Writing Time.

Developing Responding Skills

As discussed, honoring writers' voices through formal and informal sharing has a huge impact on motivation and self-efficacy. Teaching students how to thoughtfully respond to one another is also paramount since the climate of the writing community must be safe and supportive. Yet the acts of sharing and responding accomplish even more. As students listen during sharing, they learn from one another's models; as they develop responding skills they learn to reflect more thoroughly on their own writing and they benefit from their peers' useful feedback.

WHAT DID YOU HEAR?

Naturally, any responding begins with listening. If students don't listen well, they can't thoughtfully respond. Here's an idea to develop students' listening skills. As we begin the year, instead of asking students to respond when peers share, I say, "We need to develop our abilities to listen well so we can progress to responding thoughtfully to one another's work. Rather than inviting you to make comments, for now I'm going to ask just one question: 'What did you hear in _____'s writing?' If you listen well, you'll be able to para-phrase what you heard. This is the first step to becoming a productive responder."

I model to get students started, then call on volunteers. I encourage them to relay back as much as they can to get them to truly actively listen. We practice this for as long as it takes (typically six or seven days), until it is clear that students are indeed listening well. If, during the year, it seems our listening skills are go-ing awry, we go back to "What did you hear?" rather than offering responses. We continue parroting back what we heard until our skills are once again up to par.

ONGOING TEACHER MODELING OF RESPONDING SKILLS

Students need to be explicitly taught how to respond. In addition, your constant modeling is a weighty fac-tor in helping them become skillful. As I noted in the section Building Motivation by Celebrating Students' Writing (see page 17), if you haven't had much practice or are unsure what to say in response, referring to the 6+1 Traits model may be helpful. You can always comment on students' ideas, word choice, voice, orga-nization, sentence fluency, conventions, and/or presentation.

Keep your comments short and direct so as to maintain high interest and move your sharing time along. The following are examples of the types of comments and questions I might model.

- ✦ You used a topic from your life, something you know a lot about. I can tell because . . . (ideas)
- ✦ I heard specific details in your piece, such as . . . (ideas, word choice)
- ✦ As you read, I created a picture in my mind. I could see things clearly because . . . (word choice, ideas, voice)
- ✦ You know the qualities that make writing good, such as . . . (word choice, voice, organization, sentence fluency, conventions, and/or presentation). I see an example of that here: . . . (point out specific example).
- ✦ You described your characters well, for example when you wrote . . . (ideas, word choice, voice)
- ✦ You kept the readers' interest because you didn't solve the problem right away. Instead you . . . (organization, word choice, ideas)
- ✦ I heard several power words/phrases/sentences, such as . . . (word choice)
- ✦ Your lead is strong because . . . (ideas, word choice, voice, organization, sentence fluency)
- ✦ I heard some good transitional phrases, such as . . . (word choice, organization, sentence fluency)
- ✦ There was a definite beginning/middle/end. I heard . . . (ideas, word choice, organization, presentation)
- ✦ Your conclusion really works because . . . (ideas, word choice, voice, sentence fluency, organization)
- ✦ This section was very persuasive/informative/entertaining because . . . (ideas, word choice, voice, sentence fluency, organization, presentation)

- ✦ I wonder . . .
- ✦ I'm confused about . . .
- ✦ I have a question about . . .
- ✦ Tell me more about . . .

Slowly, I begin to release responsibility for responding to the class. But I never take myself totally out of the picture. I'm always right there during class sharing, eager to add to the comments students make. Teachers should continually strive to stretch thinking, and frequent modeling is an ideal way to do this.

STUDENTS RESPONDING TO ONE ANOTHER

As students take control, we begin creating a class chart titled "Keys to Thoughtful Responding." I take the lead on this, since there are several points that are the same from year to year. I also boost student ownership by including ideas they volunteer. We add to the chart over time; I don't want to overwhelm the class with too many ideas at once. You should expect responding skills to take time and practice to develop, as with any other skill. Below is the list I typically generate with the class, in the order in which ideas are presented and discussed.

Keys to Thoughtful Responding:
- ✦ must listen well
- ✦ must *think* about the writing
- ✦ can ask questions (be specific)
- ✦ can tell what you liked (be specific, use examples)
- ✦ can make suggestions (be specific)
- ✦ can ask the writer to reread
- ✦ shouldn't use the same old worn-out comments or questions ("How did you get the idea?," "How long did it take you to write?," etc. In the margins, list a few that are coming up too often in your class.)

Once we've taken ample time to develop our chart, we review it before one of our sharing times (formal or informal) about once a week. This keeps the characteristics of thoughtful responding fresh in our minds and leads to useful discussion. The weekly review is another way to promote the language of responding whenever students share with one another.

Of course, calling attention to particularly thoughtful responses is another way of promoting this behavior: "You made a specific suggestion, Cazden! How helpful! So, Lupe, do you think you *will* add another example to make your point more clear?" This is yet one more form of celebrating!

Even more ideas for organizing responding opportunities may be found in Moving on With Student Responding, page 79. What we've covered so far is a perfect place to start. Naturally, we'll also cover quick-start tips for Managing Conferences (page 81), but since those routines are set later (often beginning in week five or six), we'll stick to other short-term goals for now, namely, including short bursts of writing across the curriculum to maximize writing time and foster critical thinking.

CHAPTER 3

Quick Bursts of Writing Across the Curriculum

As shared in the introduction, your best bet for creating real writers and maximizing benefits is to combine writing workshop with daily writing across the curriculum. Let's focus there next. We use our Think Pads for many short, informal writing opportunities across the curriculum daily. It's a great way to give students extra practice writing, building their confidence while supporting thinking about content. So far, I've mentioned what I call Quick Jots. I'll elaborate below. Then, we'll explore other ways to use Think Pads.

Quick Jots

I shoot for at least three jaunts into our Think Pads each day. These are quick moments to think, jot down (one word, a few words, phrases, or sentences), question, list, brainstorm, web, respond, or note. Anytime I want to ask a question, get an opinion, or check students' understanding may be a good Think Pad time. Literally, these opportunities entail one, two, or three minutes of writing followed by very brief sharing.

To start the year, keeping my short-term goals prominent, I consciously make these opportunities very safe and very easy. I ask students to write brief notes on open-ended issues so that everyone feels rapid success. Below are a few examples. I lead off by saying, "Boys and girls, let's take just two minutes to quickly note in our Think Pads . . ."

How are your friendships developing so far this school year?
How do you feel about sitting at tables and working as teams?
Do you have questions or concerns about writing to pen pals?
Name one thing, just one thing, you learned from the assembly today.

Say what you are thinking about our classroom jobs.

Make a list of favorite things to do with your family.

Jot down your thoughts about developing a community service project for our class.

Then, there's the sharing. It's quick: "Let's take just a few minutes to share and discuss. I'm very interested in your thinking." A few volunteers share with the class. Naturally, if an issue comes up requiring extended dialogue, you might address it on the spot or table it for later. Sometimes, I end up having brief side conversations with individuals during the day to follow up. But, for the most part, strive to keep the Quick Jots very brief, so you can engage in them at least a couple of times each day. You're shooting for volume and fluency while building comfort levels with writing a lot each and every school day.

As the school year progresses, Quick Jots become more academic. Since students are accustomed to these experiences, they're undaunted by the blank page and willing to jot for a few minutes about almost anything. Again, anytime you want to check or stretch understanding, ask students to take out their Think Pads and write something related to your lesson or unit. This may involve taking quick notes on what was just learned, sketching and labeling the model just studied, or thinking beyond facts to how something learned may be applied. Here's an example where students are asked to generate questions: "As we continue our study of insects, let's take a moment to review. I'd like you to write two questions, only two, you think would be good to pose to the class to check our understanding of insects. The questions may be about anything related to our study. You have just three minutes. See what you can do!" At the same time, do continue to use Quick Jots to get students' opinions and pose open-ended queries. Finally, keep things balanced—jot for a variety of purposes.

Common Questions

"What about kids who want to write more?"

I'm not disturbed by students who continue to write as we share. After all, they can often still engage with us while finishing up or they may really be on to something at the moment. Additionally, tell students they are welcome to continue to develop their thoughts in daily writing workshop and at other free times during class. (Every year, I also have students who actually ask to take their Think Pads out for recess so they can keep working!)

"What if I'm not satisfied students are doing enough writing during these Quick Jots?"

Communicate your expectations. The best way to do this is through explicitness, modeling, and feedback during sharing. Of course, showing real interest in what students write and allowing their writing to feed a serious or excited discussion set the tone and breed success. Students are models for one another and, if you keep going with these experiences, they will push one another. You can push students to do more, too, by simply saying, "Tell me more." When they respond verbally, have them write down what was said. One more idea: If you have a student who chronically does not engage, meet with her privately to set some goals. Then be sure to follow up so she knows she's accountable and actively celebrate her small successes.

Quick Tries

Closely related to the Quick Jot is the Quick Try. The same time frame applies: one, two, or three minutes of writing in Think Pads, followed by sharing and discussion. As the name suggests, Quick Tries provide a type of practice after students have had explicit instruction toward a learning goal. They can be used for just about anything. Rather than filling in the blanks on a practice worksheet, students become accustomed to fleshing out more of their thinking with Quick Tries. Plus, again, there's the advantage of increased comfort level with the blank page, which carries over to benefits in all writing contexts. Here are some examples.

VOCABULARY QUICK TRY

Ms. Wag: *Let's look at our Vocabulary Hot List.* [That's what we call our current review list of vocabulary from across the curriculum. It consists of six to eight words. I maintain the list on the board or on a poster as a way to keep some of the most useful words we've already studied in circulation.] *Reread all the words with me.* [I point as the class reads.] *We've been working with the word* discouraged. *See it there on the list? Take out your Think Pads. I'm going to give you just thirty seconds to jot down the base word in the word* discouraged. *Just the base word. Go!* [30 seconds pass] *Okay, what's the base word in* discouraged?

Class: Courage*!*

Ms. Wag: *Right! Now, I'll give you one minute more to write down all the variations you can think of using the base word* courage. *Go!*

After one minute, we do a quick share. To clarify meanings, we use some of the variations in sentences. As sentences are made, I ask students to repeat them aloud so they practice the words to simultaneously reinforce both aural and oral representations of the word.

Or . . .

Ms. Wag: *You have thirty seconds to write a phrase or sentence using one of the words on our Hot List. Go!* [Students jot down a phrase or sentence, volunteers share aloud, the class repeats the phrase or sentence, and any clarifications about meaning or grammar are made.]

MATH QUICK TRY

Ms. WAG: (posing a math problem to the class . . .) *How many rhombuses can you make with 42 equilateral triangles? There are many different ways to solve this problem.* [See sample, right.] *We've been working on explaining our thinking and proving our answers. So, take about three minutes to jot and sketch to show your thinking.* [three minutes pass] *How might you solve the problem?*

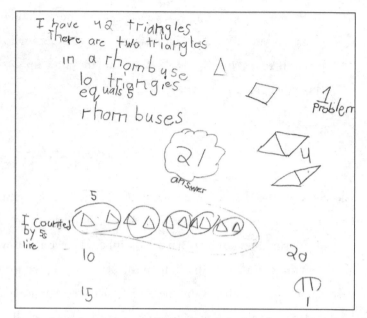

Aspen details her geometry thinking through both jotting and sketching.

SCIENCE QUICK TRY

Ms. WAG: *We've just studied the model of a cell. I'm going to cover the model so you can't see it. Take a moment and test yourselves in your Think Pads. Can you draw and label the model without looking at it? I'll give you three minutes, then you can compare with the person sitting next to you.* [I circulate as students pair-share, encouraging them to make additions and corrections. As follow-up, you might discuss how this simple exercise in writing and sketching from memory aids learning!]

WRITING CRAFT QUICK TRY

Ms. WAG: *Open your Think Pads to any page of writing. Draw a loop around a noun.* [30 seconds pass] *Now, recopy just the sentence or phrase containing that noun* [another 30 seconds pass]. *Here's what I want you to try. I'm giving you just two minutes to play with the "Power of Two" we've studied. Add two adjectives to describe the noun in your sentence or phrase. Then step back, reread what you have created, and see what you think! If you have time, try two different adjectives for the same noun and see how your sentence changes. Or, you could loop another noun from your writing and try the Power of Two again! Ready, begin!* [Again, we follow with brief sharing and discussion.]

—Adapted from Diane Murphy's *Using Six Traits Mini-Lessons to Strengthen Your Students' Writing, Grades 3–6*, a video training program from the Bureau of Education and Research (BER)

COMPREHENSION QUICK TRY

Question-Answer Relationships, or QAR (Raphael, Highfield, & Au, 2006), have received wide attention recently. Use a Quick Try to check students' knowledge of the strategy.

Ms. Wag: *Boys and girls, we've learned that the answers to "right there" questions are right there . . . in the text, literally stated, you can point right to them. We've read to the middle of this story, so take out your Think Pads and generate just two right-there questions.* [A bit of sharing allows us to clarify what right-there questions are and how to answer them.]

Or . . . another constructive Quick Try. How well have students internalized the text structure you've taught?

Ms. Wag: *We've spent a great deal of time studying narrative story structure. Take out your Think Pads and quickly list the elements of the story we just read. I'll give you three minutes. Go!*

Hint for Success with Quick Jots and Quick Tries

Be sure to keep the pace brisk. This adds to the fun and excitement (children really enjoy these short bursts!), while firmly reinforcing your expectations. Don't worry about students who sometimes don't write—this is natural. However, do meet with anyone who routinely doesn't participate, as mentioned in the Common Questions for Quick Jots.

Thinking Boxes

Thinking Boxes, like the short bursts of writing we've covered so far, are extremely versatile. You can use them to inspire thinking in any subject area. They involve more work than Quick Jots or Quick Tries and, hence, take more time. But this interactive method will give you impressive learning results! Here's how they work.

Students fold the next page in their Think Pads in half vertically. Then, they draw a line horizontally through the middle of the page so they have four boxes. They repeat the horizontal line on the back if more than four boxes are needed. They number the boxes.

As you read something, work through a lesson, complete an experiment, or are engaged in some other learning event, stop periodically so students can process what they are learning/thinking through writing. They work in one box at a time, under your direction, then quickly share. The cycle repeats: Continue to stop, think, write, and share throughout the experience. Brain research tells us we can only take in so much at a time without stopping to actively process. Thinking Boxes are an example of best practice, given this research. Best of all, kids love it!

THINKING BOXES EXAMPLE: GRADE 4

A fourth-grade teacher recently asked me to read an expository article about the water cycle with her class. She wondered how to help students more deeply process the ideas in the article so they'd learn the most important points and retain what was read. I suggested a Quick Write (see page 38), but they had completed one the day before following a math investigation. Another great solution: Thinking Boxes!

Here, I modeled thinking, jotting and sketching as a class of fourth graders and I actively worked through an article on the water cycle using Thinking Boxes.

Since this class didn't have Think Pads, I had the fourth graders fold a blank piece of white paper into four squares, numbering them 1 to 4. As we worked through the article, I stopped and allowed them time to process (just two to three minutes) by having them jot and sketch (if desired) in a square, or Thinking Box. We then quickly talked about their ideas and continued reading, pausing three additional times to work in the remaining Thinking Boxes. Since this was their first time using the strategy, I folded a poster-size paper and modeled up front on the board (see my example, above).

On the first page of the article, there were several important statistics key to understanding why the water cycle is important. After I read this page aloud while students followed on their copies, I said,

> Boys and girls, I'm going to give you just a minute to jot a few words, phrases, or sentences to help you remember the important statistics we just read about fresh, salt, and frozen water. You might add a sketch to help you remember what you're learning, but you must write. Do that in box number 1.

After a minute or so, I asked volunteers to share. We reviewed the statistics aloud and one child shared a sketch of Earth with arrows pointing to the oceans (which she labeled "97% salt water") and ice caps (which she labeled "2% frozen"). Then we read on. The next section of the article detailed how the water cycle works. After reading, I said,

> Think for a minute and put together the information we just read. Why won't the water cycle work without the sun? Take a few moments to jot a few words, phrases, or sentences about that in box number 2. What do you think? Remember, you may also add a sketch, but you must write.

The answer to this question was not explicitly stated in the text. After about two minutes, I opened it up for sharing. I found most students did not fully understand this element of the water cycle, so I explained further and modeled writing my answer. I invited students to take a moment to clarify their thinking in box number 2, if needed. We read on. In box 3, I asked students to jot and sketch about a time they personally experienced condensation or evaporation. Several students shared: one about sitting in a hotel hot tub, another about seeing the steam rise from a pot of soup, and another about holding a glass of iced lemonade on a hot day. After reading the final section of the article, I said,

> *Now that we've completed our reading, let's go back to the title. This article is called "Water—More Precious Than Gold," and we find Grandpa repeats this idea throughout. What do you think Grandpa meant by this: "Water is more precious than gold"? Think for a moment. Then, jot what you think he meant in box number 4."*

While students worked, I completed my box on the board and, again, we quickly discussed their thinking.

I hope this example gives you a window into the power of Thinking Boxes! Did it take longer to read the article, complete the Thinking Boxes, and share than just to read it and ask questions? Yes, a bit more time was required. But what do you think students really took away from this experience? Were they more engaged? Did they have the chance to just tune out? In fact, in this particular instance, I was curious to check students' retention and understanding. So, a full week later, I asked the same fourth graders to complete a Quick Write about what they had learned from the article. Most students included several points we had reviewed in the Thinking Boxes! This was even more impressive when the teacher shared the fact that they had not done further study of the water cycle since my last visit.

Thinking Boxes enables teachers to gather valuable information about what students are really learning. Then they can clarify and elaborate on points right when confusions or gaps in understanding occur! What great responsive teaching! Additionally, Thinking Boxes is another teaching/learning method that communicates how we value students' thinking and voices. This is a powerful way to increase engagement.

Sketching vs. Drawing

When you first work with a class, you might need to define the difference between *sketching* and *drawing*. I do this by modeling: I "sketch" a dog on the board (using few lines and details), then "draw" a dog (taking much more time, using more lines and details). We talk about the difference. Since we spend only a few minutes in each Thinking Box, students readily get the idea of why sketching is important.

THINKING BOXES PROMOTE ALL KINDS OF THINKING!

Before we move on, let's examine the kind of thinking asked of students in each box of the water cycle lesson.

- In the first box: Students took quick notes on facts specifically stated in the article
- In the second box: Students were asked to synthesize information to draw a conclusion
- In the third box: Students connected to personal experience, essentially attaching new learning to their existing schemas for water
- In the fourth box: They were asked to draw an inference about a quote from the text

Wow! That's a great deal of higher-level thinking, all done within a few minutes of jotting, sketching, and sharing, followed up with brief discussion. You might certainly ease your students into using Thinking Boxes by posing simple, literal questions or just reviewing content as you go, but I'm betting you'll be impressed with what they can do and how easy it is to get into all kinds of higher-level thinking. Remember, the sharing and modeling for one another is paramount to achieving growth in thinking skills.

In the end, Thinking Boxes are a worthwhile alternative to asking students to read, study, or experience something and answer questions on their own afterward. In fact, this school year, I shared the technique of using Thinking Boxes with a good reading-teacher friend of mine who works with intervention groups. She used them with her small groups of strugglers for a few weeks and was absolutely raving about it! She couldn't believe how engaged the students were, even though she was asking them to do similar things in the boxes that they previously were doing begrudgingly at the end of reading selections. She concluded the idea of "jotting" really freed them up and the option of sketching was a huge motivator. She felt breaking up the reading/learning experience was helpful and that giving students a short time limit to work in the boxes was key. Additionally, she was amazed how the quick sharing and discussion maintained their excitement! She was sold on the procedure and asked me to fill her in on other "quick writing things that work for student learning!"

THE MANY USES OF THINKING BOXES

One of the beauties of Thinking Boxes is the versatility of the strategy. You can use it to get your students writing about/thinking through almost anything. Here are some ideas.

- Have students stop and jot in Thinking Boxes to practice using comprehension strategies as you read a book, article, or selection aloud or complete some form of shared or guided reading. You'll be impressed how you can review, clarify, and concretely practice the comprehension strategies you teach. Example: Box 1, make a prediction; Box 2, summarize what's happened so far; Box 3, draw an inference; Box 4, form a question; Box 5, synthesize: What do you think the author's message is?

- Use Thinking Boxes to process anything students are viewing/hearing. Stop a DVD, PowerPoint presentation, or newscast in several places to allow students to process through writing.

- Use Thinking Boxes to review the steps of a science experiment as you work through the experience. You might have students describe the experiment's purpose in the first box, create a hypothesis in another, share their thinking about the steps in the experiment in the next few boxes . . . and list their conclusions in the last box.

- Use Thinking Boxes in math to have students process each of the steps to completing an algorithm or think through each of the steps they're using to solve a problem.

- Use Thinking Boxes to plan an event or presentation: What will you do/say first, second, third, and so on? How will you conclude, sum up?

- Use Thinking Boxes as a prewriting strategy. Example: Outline your persuasive letter. In the first box, think through your greeting and opening statement. In the second box, jot a few words about your first point and list examples. In the third box, think through your second point and examples, and so on. Then, in the last box, jot notes to help you craft a powerful closing for your letter.

Thinking Boxes as Formative Assessment

Thinking Boxes can also be used as a tool for formative assessment. Say you want to see how your students are doing using the comprehension strategies you've taught. Read something aloud and ask them to employ a strategy in each box (still simply jotting words, phrases, or sentences to respond, adding sketches, if desired). Tell them, "Today, you'll be turning in your Thinking Boxes so I can take a closer look at how you're doing. Since I want to evaluate your individual work, we won't be sharing as we go."

Variation: What Are You Thinking?

I call this variation on Thinking Boxes "What Are You Thinking?" I use it for the same kinds of activities; however, each time I stop, I repeat one open-ended question: "What are you thinking?" Students jot and sketch in each box, as usual. When they share, I ask the class, "What kind of thinking was that?" This enables us to discuss, review, and practice a host of thinking strategies such as predicting, inferring, categorizing, hypothesizing, evaluating, concluding, synthesizing, elaborating, even experimenting. I bet you'll be surprised by some of the advanced thinking going on in students' brains and how it comes out in these quick writing opportunities. Again, this is great student-to-student modeling! And what a perfect way to demonstrate how we are always employing those same thinking strategies across the curriculum!

Quick Writes

I involve students in Quick Writes (Elbow, 1973) when I want to give them more time to develop their thinking through writing. The big difference here is that Quick Writes allow for sustained writing in one shot. Like the other techniques, you can quick-write about anything: experiences, content, reading. They can occur before, during, or after experiencing, studying content, or reading. Typically, I give students seven to ten minutes to write based on a prompt. I set a timer to make sure we adhere to the time limit. I write while they write and simply put my hand up (HALT!) if a student gets out of her seat or tries to talk to me or her peers during the Quick Write. Several examples follow.

Before I start the timer, I frame the prompt and review the rules (see box below). Since we quick-write frequently (at least twice a week), I have a poster listing the rules.

Once, my second graders and I did a Quick Write after reading *Hope for the Flowers* (Paulus, 1972). This story is about two caterpillars trying to make their way in the world. One follows her heart, the other blindly does what everybody else is doing. When we finished the novella, I asked students to make connections to their own experiences and write about them in their Think Pads. "Let's take a few minutes for a Quick Write. Thinking about what we learned from this story, I'd like you to write about a time you followed your heart and did the right thing, just like Yellow [a main character]. If you can't think of such a time, you might write about a time you did what others around you were doing, even though you knew it was wrong, just like Stripe [a main character]. If you are having trouble with either of these, you might write about something that caught your attention in the book *Hope for the Flowers*. Okay, you have seven minutes to write." (See student examples on the next page.)

When beginning the year, keep your prompts open-ended to ensure success. You might widen the possibilities even further after framing your prompt by adding something like I did above, "If you are

Rules for a Quick Write

- Everyone writes.
- Stay on topic.
- There is no single right answer.
- If you don't know what to write about, write: "I don't know what to write, I don't know what to write" over and over until this jogs your mind into action.
- Continue writing until time is up. If you finish early, reread your response, reflect, and make changes or additions, until time is up. (With younger students, you might add the option of sketching as part of their response. But, writing *must* accompany the sketch.)
- You *may* share your writing, but you are not required to do so.
- You *may* respond to the Quick Writes of others once they are shared.

having trouble . . . write about something that caught your attention in the book."

You might also jot something on the board to remind students of the prompt(s). When the timer goes off, I say, "Time is up. You may not be done, and that's okay. Let's stop now and hear some responses. Feel free to give each other feedback as we go. Who would like to share?" Volunteers stand and share their pieces. I share my writing, too, and model appropriate responses (paraphrasing, questioning, and relating), as always.

SECOND-GRADE STUDENTS' SAMPLE QUICK WRITES AND MY FEEDBACK

for *Hope for the Flowers*

I was at my friend's house and he had some Kool-Aid. He told me to eat it from the pack. My heart told me not to do it! My friend did it and he threw up! –Garrett

Ms. WAG: *Garrett, you've done a great job of staying on the topic. You even used some of the language from the prompt when writing your answer, like "My heart told me not to do it!" I love how you used a real example from your life. The consequence for your friend shows how important the life's lesson from the story is: "he threw up!"*

One time, I was at my house having a sleepover. My friend who was sleeping over said, "Want to doorbell ditch?" I said, "I don't think that's a good idea." She said, "Come on, you know you want to." "No, I don't." So, she said, "Okay, I'll do it with somebody else another time." I listened to my heart. –McCall

Ms. WAG: *I really appreciate how you used dialogue to show your example. You've crafted the dialogue well because it sounds like real kids talking—for example, "Come on, you know you want to." Your example here also shows how standing up for yourself can work. You flatly said, "No, I don't." The message in the story comes out (you're right on topic here!), because you followed your heart and your friend gave in, saying, "Okay, I'll do it with somebody else another time." Great example, McCall. One thing I'm thinking is, you ended with "I listened to my heart." I still want to know how you felt about the experience. And are you and your friend still friends? You could write more about that."*

MORE QUICK-WRITE EXAMPLES

A sixth-grade teacher and his class are finishing a unit on bacteria: "As we complete our study of bacteria, let me give you about seven minutes for a Quick Write. Take out your Think Pads and briefly sum up the most important things you've learned." When time is up, he asks students to turn in their Think Pads, laying them facedown open to the current page. Later in the day, he quickly glances through the papers to determine students' knowledge and what he needs to reteach or clarify before the unit test. As he passes back notebooks he says, "I realize I didn't give you the opportunity to share aloud after this Quick Write. Instead, I reviewed each person's writing myself. Here is what I learned." He launches into a few critical re-teaching points.

A third-grade teacher has been studying story structure with her class: "For our Quick Write today, I'd like you to write a summary of the story we just read. Please organize it according to the narrative story structure we've been studying, since it follows the structure exactly. So, begin your summary stating who the characters are and where the story takes place. Then, be sure to detail the problem and the attempts to solve it. Finally, include how the problem was resolved. I'll be writing while you write."

One year, in the spring of second grade, I asked my students to do a Quick Write about life cycles. I left the prompt very open-ended: "We've been studying life cycles for several weeks now. We've watched the cycle of the painted lady butterfly firsthand. We've also keenly observed and researched about our tadpole visitors. So, today, we'll do a Quick Write about life cycles. You might write something about the butterflies or the tadpoles or about your general knowledge of life cycles. You can use any form you'd like—a letter, a list of facts, a poem—but be sure to focus on your understanding of life cycles." At right is an example of what one of my second graders produced. It was hard to choose just one since so many children produced amazing results! In fact, we were all so impressed we decided to bind our Quick Writes into a classroom collection. A volunteer typed them up (including mine) and corrected spelling errors, then students illustrated and we put them into a book. It was a hot item during take-home check-out! What a superb way to culminate a unit of study!

Just to throw in a social studies example, we did the same experience when we finished up our study of Dr. Martin Luther King, Jr. Students responded to what we'd learned through Quick Writes. Their writing

tade-Pole changing

When your a tade-pole you're like a dote with a tial. Then pop! It seems like legs poped out! Then pop again!! then your arms plop out.. While all that is happening... your tail is shrinking!!!! When the tail is gone, your a... Frog!

Savanah's Quick Write: a free-style poem about the life cycle of a frog.

was so good, we again created a class book to celebrate! I'll never forget that one student began his response with the words: "I feel shame and madness." Powerful! You go, second graders!

One last example: A fourth-grade teacher in my school opens each day with a Quick Write. Her main goal is to increase students' fluency since the majority of her incoming students are very reluctant to write. She frames a prompt related to what's happening in the classroom, things they are studying or reading, or one typically known as a "story starter" (e.g., "If I had twelve sisters . . ."). She uses the rules I've outlined and pulls sticks to manage sharing (see page 22). Without doing anything more with connected writing (she doesn't have a Writing Workshop and she follows the basal reading/spelling program which doesn't incorporate much writing), look at the results! Below are two Quick Write samples from Emilio, a struggling fourth grader. The first, from November, shows that the only thing he accomplished with his time was an attempt to write down the prompt. The sample reflects low esteem and a lack of writing skills. The second, from March, shows a huge increase in fluency and skill!

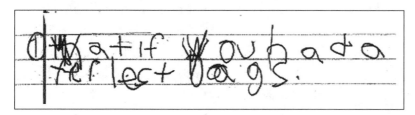

Emilio's Quick Write sample from November: "What if you had a fearless day"

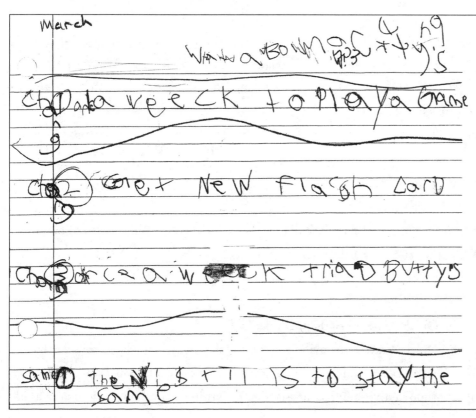

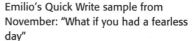

Five months later, Emilio wrote this Quick Write in response to the prompt: "Tell me what you think should stay the same and what you think should change about our Kindergarten Buddy time." (This class met with their kindergarten buddies three times each week). He wrote:

Change ① once a week to play a game

Change ② get new flash card

Change ③ once a week triad buddies

Same ④ the Versatiles stay the same

QUICK WRITES HELP STUDENTS PREPARE FOR HIGH-STAKES TESTING

Some teachers use the Quick Write strategy to help their students prepare to answer prompts in essay form on tests. They stick with the ten-minute writing time, but focus their sharing and feedback on how well students stayed true to the prompt and formed their opinions or arguments. The Quick Write format makes frequent practice and specific feedback more accessible for many students since they're not required to prepare a full-blown, completed essay. One note of caution here is to ease into using Quick Writes for this purpose only after you've created a strong, comfortable environment and your other short-term goals are met. Then, continue to use Quick Writes for other purposes as well.

Side Note: If one of your teaching goals is to help students learn to respond to prompts, be sure to use some of your writing workshop mini-lessons to explicitly address the skills they'll need in order to be successful. You should include specific lessons targeting strategies like using transitions, organizing writing, using examples and anecdotes to support points, and crafting persuasive language. Employ the techniques covered in the upcoming Workshop Essentials section like Modeled Writing, Peer Revision Activities, Circling Skills We Know, and the Quality Writing Notebook.

Important Anecdote: Fourth Graders Have No Thoughts?!

As a literacy coach, I often do model lessons. Recently, I modeled a Quick Write in a fourth-grade classroom. The teacher was reading *Stone Fox* (Gardiner, 1992) aloud to the class. They were about three-fourths of the way through the novel. I talked to the group about the procedure for a Quick Write, reviewed the rules, and asked them to write about what they thought of Little Willy's actions thus far. (If you don't know the book, Little Willy bravely tries to save his sick grandfather's farm from foreclosure.) After about eight minutes, we shared. I was shocked to find only two students actually recorded anything having to do with *their thoughts* about Little Willy! (Only a few shared aloud, but I confirmed this later after reviewing their work.) Instead, they simply recounted the events in the story. The only conclusion I could draw was these students weren't asked to express their own thoughts very often. How sad.

Common Questions

"What do you do with the Quick Writes once they're done?"

You don't have to follow up Quick Writes with anything. After the sharing, you might be completely done with the experience. Or, you can extend an invitation for students to do additional work on a Quick Write. There's always time to develop something further in Writing Workshop. Additionally, as in the life cycle example, you might bind Quick Writes into a class book a few times throughout the year.

Sometimes, you may want the class to keep their Think Pads open to the current Quick Write and turn them in for your review, as with the sixth-grade bacteria example. This is an efficient way to check on knowledge and participation.

Be sure the dated Quick Writes remain in students' Think Pads, so you can assess their progress as writers. You should see growth over time in the volume they produce, the quality of their ideas and abilities to organize their thinking, their spelling and their use of conventions (especially so if you combine the frequent quick bursts with daily Writing Workshop, as I'm advocating). In fact, since all the quick bursts (Quick Jots, Quick Tries, and Thinking Boxes included) should be dated, any of these might be used to assess progress. Particularly useful samples might be tagged with sticky notes or torn from the pad and placed in portfolios.

"What do the quick bursts of writing across the curriculum have to do with success in Writing Workshop?"

In a word: everything! Just as with reading, the number of opportunities for practice and the volume of work matters greatly for increasing students' skill levels. Quick bursts add variety to students' experience and build their understanding of writing's varied purposes. They gain perspective about the value of writing as a tool for learning. Additionally, as explained in the Quick-Start Tips (see page 9), the quick bursts provide different modes of writing with different benefits. Naturally, all the added writing and sharing brought about by the quick bursts contributes to building a serious-minded writing community and, again, makes writing just part of what we do every day. These advantages spill over to make the writing workshop flourish even more.

Can a teacher hold a successful writing workshop without the quick bursts? Yes. I did it for years. But why not give your students the power of the full learning potential writing holds? If we can learn more effectively through writing, we should use it as a learning tool throughout the school day. And, indeed, writing leads to better learning in a myriad of ways, including deepening engagement, understanding, and retention.

With the basics in place, we'll take a closer look at how to keep writing workshop running smoothly in Part II.

> **"In classrooms—including those in high-poverty schools—where student achievement is high, reading and writing are routinely linked, and students have a great many writing opportunities across the curriculum."**
>
> —Knapp (1995)

Part II: Workshop Essentials

CHAPTER 4:

Modeled Writing

The techniques described in the following chapters make up the meat of my writing workshop. They are my best lessons—tried-and-true ideas—that I've continually labored over to make better and better. Like the quick bursts, they are versatile strategies you'll find highly effective for increasing student achievement.

Day-by-Day Outline

Modeled Writing can be used whenever you want to motivate writing, teach any objective related to process or craft, or introduce a new genre or assignment. Very simply, it is "showing, not telling" at its finest. The teaching is still explicit: We start by explaining what we're doing, why we're doing it, and how we're doing it, but then we go on to model it, thinking aloud as we engage in writing right in front of the students! Sound scary? It might be at first, but it's truly worth the leap (plus, in the Common Questions section on page 52, I'll share some ways to ease yourself into the process so you can comfortably build experience).

During my first year teaching writing, when I "taught" the writing process, I told students the

Modeled Writing for Short- and Long-Term Goals

Modeled Writing can be used to work on short- or long-term goals. For example, you might employ Modeled Writing as one of your first (short-term) techniques for inspiring children to write about something from their lives. You might later use Modeled Writing in support of your long-term goal of demonstrating specifics about compare-and-contrast pieces.

steps and listed them on the board. Then, we took a day to "do" each step. When I introduced a new genre or writing assignment, I told students what to do step by step or with an outline. Of course, some students got it and some didn't. Now, if I want to teach report writing, for example, I post a blank piece of chart paper and start writing while thinking aloud. This alone has great impact because I'm communicating that writing is important to me, something I value and enjoy, and that I am part of the classroom community of learners/writers.

The outline below is a guide to the steps I follow for Modeled Writing experiences.

DAY 1

STEP ONE: Tell your idea to students. Discuss your intended audience and purpose (to learn, inform, entertain, or persuade). If desired, quickly jot notes on a piece of chart paper (or prewrite in another form, like a web, list, or outline).

STEP TWO: Begin crafting your piece in draft form (see box at right). Write for just a few minutes. Read and reread your emerging text. Make changes and fix any errors you notice as you go. Refer back to the prewrite (if applicable) as you proceed. Think aloud as you write.

STEP THREE: Explicitly debrief with students. Ask, "What specifically did you see me do as a writer?" Record responses directly on the draft with a different-color marker (this way, you can go back and review strategies).

DAY 2

STEP ONE: Review your prewriting (if applicable). Comment on parts you have already included in your draft and where you might be going next. Then, reread your draft. Make any revisions to the content and changes to the form. Talk through where you're headed next and add to your piece. Think aloud as you go. Write for just a few minutes, again, making changes as you read and reread.

STEP TWO: Explicitly debrief with students. Ask, "What specifically did you see me do as a writer?" Record responses directly on the draft with a different-color marker.

Drafting

To "draft" still means to do our best work. I don't like the term "sloppy copy" because it denotes we're just recording things any old way—perhaps haphazardly. I teach my students to *always* do their best—best spelling, best use of conventions, and so on (even when we're recording things quickly just to get our ideas down). My mantra is: "Use what you know." We call it a draft because it's a piece in process. Drafting involves reading and rereading as we write and making revisions and editing as we go. This is a recursive, not linear, process (you'll get a better sense of this in the scripted lesson examples that follow).

DAYS 3, 4, 5 . . .

Repeat steps one and two from Day 2. Take as many days as necessary to complete your piece, or work through your piece up to the point of your goal (see box at right).

LASTLY

Decide if your purpose includes publishing your piece. If so, begin the process in front of students, demonstrating how you use your draft as a blueprint. Finish the product outside of class and celebrate in the Author's Chair, inviting student comments. Add your piece to the classroom library or bulletin board. Just think: If you published only one piece a year, over time you'd have a robust collection to share with students!

> ### Focus on the Goal
>
> You DON'T have to complete every piece of Modeled Writing you start. Simply write to the point of your goal. For example, if your goal is to help your students write stronger leads, you might do a series of Modeled Writing experiences where you only *begin* pieces.

In my classroom, Modeled Writing occurs as a series of ongoing mini-lessons, each lasting about ten minutes, to open the workshop. It may take several consecutive days to complete an experience. When I am finished each day and have explicitly debriefed with students, we begin Open Writing Time when everyone works on assignments or choice pieces from their Think Pads and writing workshop folders.

MODELED WRITING TO DEMONSTRATE THE WRITING PROCESS

Before you begin a Modeled Writing experience, you must define your purpose. Let's say you're starting a new school year and you want students to get to know the writing process. You might begin with a common form of writing: the personal narrative. Here's what such a Modeled Writing demonstration would sound like in my classroom.

> *We are all writers! We all have stories to tell. This year, you'll be invited to write lots of stories, poems, letters, and informational or opinion pieces. Today, while you listen and watch, I'm going to begin my first piece for the year! You'll see me write down some ideas, choose one, brainstorm some notes, and begin to write my story. Watch what I do and we'll talk about what you saw. You'll observe many strategies you can use as writers!*
>
> *I have a couple of ideas. I learned to ride a four-wheeler this summer. It was quite an adventure! I could write about that* [jots a note about the four-wheeler at the top of the chart paper]. *Another idea I have is to write about going to the desert to hunt for geodes* [jots another note]. *I'm glad I wrote both of these down, so I don't forget my ideas. But today I feel like*

writing about the four-wheeler. I think I have more to say about that right now and I feel more excited about it as my first topic. Plus, since you'll be my audience, I think this topic will be entertaining for you.

Let me tell you about learning to ride. First of all, I had to be fitted for a helmet [jots note: "fitted for helmet"]. I didn't like this at all because I felt like I couldn't breathe freely inside it [jots note: "couldn't breathe"]. Then, my friend showed me how to operate the machine. There was a lot to remember, and he went kind of fast, so I felt nervous. I didn't know if I understood it all [jots note: "steps to operate (fast, nervous)"]. Next, he said, "You can do it. Just give it a try!"

That's all I want to tell you for now. Let me add a few more notes to my prewriting list, though, because I think I have a plan for my writing and I don't want to forget it [jots notes: "Troy said, 'You can do it! Just give it a try!' First try. Second try. And, I was off! Adventures over the hills"].

Okay, I have some notes about my general idea, but now I want to start my draft. Let's see. I'm not sure what I'll call this piece, so I'm going to skip the title for now. I want to create an interesting lead or beginning sentence for my story so that people will want to read it. That can be hard to do. But I know I can give it a try and always come back and change it if I want. Hmmmm . . . [pausing, then writing] "One long, hot summer day." No, wait a minute, maybe I could start with a question. "What do you do on a hot summer day? Go four-wheeling, of course!" Yes, I like how that sounds. So, I'll cross out my other sentence [crossing out "One long, hot summer day"] with a single line so I can still refer to it later if I want.

Now, let me reread and move on [rereads, then writes while talking]. **"First, you have to learn how! I began my adventure in learning to ride with trying on helmets."** Now, wait. I can make that sound more interesting. It seemed like the helmet experience went on forever. Let me change my words to better capture what it was like. I'll cross out the s in helmets and make it [writing] "helmet after helmet after helmet." That description will help readers get a clearer picture in their minds. I want to reread as I go—good writers are always doing that—to

Modeled Writing, including topic generating, prewriting, notes, and beginning to draft

make sure I'm saying what I want to say and that I like how it sounds. [rereads from the beginning] So far, I like it. I want to include the part I told you about and wrote on my notes about how I felt I couldn't breathe. [writing] "All of them seemed to shut down my breathing." No, that sounds too technical and it doesn't seem to go with the voice I have going.

Modeled Writing: drafting continued

Let me try something else. [crossing out and writing] "I felt like I was swimming in them! I could hardly breathe! But, the first rule of 4-wheeling is you have to be safe. Wearing a helmet is not optional!"

Well, that's all the time I have for today. I'll come back to this, reread, and add tomorrow. I'm glad I have my notes to guide me. Before I turn the time over to you to write, let's talk for a minute. What specifically did you see me do or say as a writer? I'll write down your ideas in a different-color marker so we can talk about the things good writers do.

This example shows a short, introductory lesson. Certainly, teachers who are new to this process may start smaller, modeling for even five minutes per session. As you can see, it's amazing how much modeling you can do in such a short period of time. Imagine if you used this technique frequently! The ongoing modeling will include repeating and demonstrating again and again the strategies good writers use. This way, the strategies really sink in. The last step of asking, "What specifically did you see me do or say as a writer?" makes the strategies explicit and concrete. Making notes in the text helps clarify where, when, and why strategies are employed and allows you to refer back to them as needed.

When you first ask this question, though, students might have trouble answering. If this is the case, model what you're looking for. Point to a spot in your draft and comment, "Did you see what I did right here? I stopped and reread from the beginning. How do you think that strategy is helpful to writers?"

In the scripted example above, students noted that I:

✦ used a topic from my life experience

✦ wrote notes to myself about the story before I started (pre-wrote a sequential list)

✦ skipped the title

✦ changed the first sentence and crossed it out

- worked on the lead to make it interesting
- reread over and over to check if it sounded right
- changed the word *helmets* to *helmet after helmet after helmet* to help readers picture it in their minds (worked on word choice)
- used exclamation marks
- changed a sentence to keep the voice of the piece consistent

I always seem to have more things in mind than what students notice. So, I ask some questions like "When I got stuck here, what did I do?" to push and guide the strategy debriefing. I close the lesson by saying, "Wow! You noticed many strategies good writers use. Be sure to use them in your own writing. If you're not sure how yet, don't worry. I'll keep demonstrating and we'll keep discussing what writers do. Plus, we'll have time to write and practice every day!"

MODELED WRITING TO INTRODUCE A NEW GENRE

To introduce a new genre, I follow the same daily outline. Before we begin our writing work, though, we read plenty of examples. I immerse students in the genre with read-alouds, shared reading, and baskets of choice books for independent reading. This is essential. As Cazden (1991) says, "Children would not learn to speak a language they do not hear; how do we expect them to learn to write forms they do not read?" Sometimes, we keep a list of characteristics we notice in the genre as we read the examples. Then, I begin the Modeled Writing process.

> *We've been reading all kinds of poetry. We've noticed how some poems rhyme and some don't. We've also noticed how many poems use just a few words and that authors seem careful about how they place their words on the page: moving down the page, breaking the lines to create pauses and rhythms, and leaving lots of white space. I'm sure we still have a lot to discover about poetry. But I'm very excited and I'd like to try writing my own poem now. Watch and listen carefully because you might want to try one yourself.*
>
> *Okay* [placing a piece of chart paper on the board], *first I'd better think about what my poem could be about. I have to go to the dentist tomorrow. I could write about visits to the dentist* [jots down "dentist"]. *Maybe I could call my poem "Ouch!"* [jots down "Ouch!"]. *Everyone has to go to the dentist, and many people have strong feelings about such visits. So, that might be a poem readers would relate to. What else? Hmmmm . . . I love my cat. I could write about her. Remember all those animal poems we read? Seems like Quincy would make a good topic for a poem* [jots down "Quincy"]. *Gee, that makes me think of my cat Snydley, who died last year. I could write a poem about him* [jots down "Snydley"]. *I could even dedicate it*

to him. All of these seem like good ideas. Let me try something for Snydley. I can always write about the dentist or my cat Quincy later.

I think I'll call it [writing] *"To Snydley" because I wish I could share it with him. Let's see, I think I'll start by describing him.* [begins to write.]

> **Lots of soft**
>
> **black hair**
>
> **all I have**
>
> **left of you.**

Let me reread that part [rereads]. *I think I should change the word* lots. *It's a word that gets overused by writers, plus it's very vague. Let me try something more specific* [crossing out "lots"]. *Maybe* tufts. *Yes,* tufts [writing] *works because I kept some little clumps of his hair when we buried him. Let me reread again and see what else comes to mind.* [rereading]

> **Tufts of soft**
>
> **black hair**
>
> **all I have**
>
> **left of you**
>
> [*adding*] **warm, beautiful cat.**

Practice Strategy Debriefing

Take a moment to practice. Reread the poetry think-aloud and jot some notes: What writing strategies might students notice? What might you ask them to attend to?

I want to make it sound loving. I think "warm, beautiful cat" works here. Plus, it lets the reader know what I'm talking about—my cat. Okay, I started with Snydley's physical description. Maybe now I can include some of his funny behaviors. I'll give that a try. He did many funny things. By including them in the poem, I'll always remember them. [begins to write]

> **So loud, so loud**
>
> **and loving**
>
> **paws around my neck**
>
> **and a cold-nose kiss.**

He was always meowing and . . . he was loud! He was very affectionate. I used the word loving *instead of* affectionate *because I like how it sounds right there by the word* loud. *That is an example of alliteration—it sounds nice because several of the words begin with the same*

sound, /lllll/. I loved it when he'd give me a wet Snydley-kiss. Okay, let me reread. [rereads]
See, boys and girls, if you write a poem, you might do as I've done here, jot something about the
physical description of your topic, then think about things your topic does. Writing this poem
really makes me miss my cat. I want to cry and I want to smile at the same time! Poetry can
bring out many emotions.

Of course, my poem could continue from there. But, after a few minutes composing, I stop, debrief, and process for the day, asking, "What specifically did you see me do as a writer?" Again, I note the students' responses, then invite them to begin experimenting with the genre. The following day, I come back to my piece, reread, revise, and edit if necessary, and continue drafting. You might follow up by planning a class book of poetry and assigning a publishing due date.

MODELED WRITING TO INTRODUCE A NEW WRITING ASSIGNMENT

I often reflect on how some of my junior high and high school teachers gave writing assignments: "Everybody write a persuasive article on why slavery should have been abolished. Use three sources. Make sure it's at least two pages long. It's due Wednesday." I know I could have learned so much about the writing process and completed such assignments with more ease and success if Modeled Writing had been part of my teachers' repertoires. Imagine the power of beginning the experience with the steps of the daily routine I've shared. Teachers who do so gain an appreciation for their students as writers and the complexities of the writing process. They also clarify the steps involved in completing the assignment and help their students truly understand what is needed to do a good job.

Keep in mind that with such assignments, even a little bit of modeling is better than none. You might begin by discussing your audience and purpose, making notes about your main points, referring back to sources, then drafting the introduction and first paragraph. This may be enough to get your students cooking. Again, not all Modeled Writing has to involve completing all steps of the writing process.

Common Questions

"This sounds scary. I'm not confident enough to write in front of students. Can I still do Modeled Writing?"

Yes! There are degrees of modeling. You can ease in with less exposure in front of the class. For example, you can work on prewriting and drafting outside of class, make an overhead of your work (or use a document camera to show it), and discuss the steps you took as you wrote. Just be sure to show all your work (leave cross-outs, arrows, carets, etc.), so students can see it and you can easily discuss your strategies. As with other Modeled Writing lessons, do a little bit each day so it's not overwhelming.

"What if I get in front of students and don't know what to write or think aloud about?"

When this happens, take heart. Thinking aloud about being stuck, confused, or unsure is great modeling. Your students experience the same things! These are all part of the creativity and complexity of writing. You can always invite students to help: "I'm completely

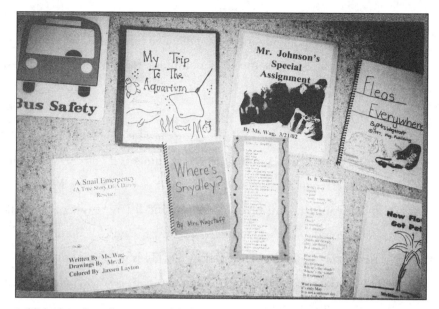

Published products from my Modeled Writing lessons, including fiction, nonfiction, and poetry.

stuck here. Can anybody think of . . . ? What I might do next? What's another word for . . . ? How might I say this differently? What's a way I can transition to my next idea? What's another word that would help me spell . . . ?" Trust me, they'll often surprise you! Besides, this shows the value of peer input and response. Remember, as you do more and more Modeled Writing, you'll feel more and more comfortable. Know that it's okay to learn as you go; that's exactly what your students are doing! When the going gets tough, remember how Donald Graves (quoted in Murray, 1995) responded when asked about the most important thing teachers should do when teaching writing. He said, "Write yourself."

"If I'm doing Modeled Writing for my mini-lessons, what about all the other mini-lessons I need to do? When do I fit it all in?"

Using your mini-lesson time for Modeled Writing does not mean you exclude other mini-lessons. I use the time in between Modeled Writing experiences to get in other critical mini-lessons. For example, I may work on a draft of a letter for three days, then do other types of mini-lessons for two weeks before moving to another bit of Modeled Writing.

Also, consider your content area. If you're having students work on describing the animal habitats they're studying, your Modeled Writing lesson can actually occur during science time!

"How long should a Modeled Writing experience take?"

Again, this depends on your purpose. You may wish to complete the first three paragraphs of an essay so your students get a feel for an assignment. This might involve three or four mini-lessons. You may write a limerick, share it aloud, and be done in two mini-lessons. To complete a whole story, it often takes me a week of mini-lessons, sometimes a bit more. Each experience is different.

Follow Up

◆ Look for examples of students using the strategies you've modeled. At the very least, celebrate these aloud as you circulate. Better yet, ask students if you can share and celebrate their work with the whole class on the document camera. If you do enough Modeled Writing, you'll be amazed how much your students revise! Watching and listening to a model makes all the difference because students come to understand why and how to revise. It becomes a natural part of their daily process.

◆ Keep your Modeled Writing examples. This way, you can use them throughout the year to review skills, strategies, and genres. When a student is stuck, coming back to these concrete examples can be extremely helpful.

CHAPTER 5

Revision Strategies That Work

Once students are happily writing and your short-term goals are in full swing, turn your attention to longer-term objectives like practicing revision, editing, spelling, and studying the characteristics of quality writing. Additionally, you may want to broaden students' responding opportunities and get into "official" writing conferences.

Peer Revision Activities

All writing teachers are challenged to find ways to help students understand and use revision. Modeling the recursive nature of writing goes a long way toward making this goal attainable. I've developed another teaching strategy that works wonders as well: Peer Revision. Through Peer Revision, students get concrete practice in reading and rereading pieces, thinking about the content, and making meaningful changes in a nonthreatening, socially supportive atmosphere.

To begin, students find a partner and read the paragraph(s) I have prepared and copied for them. After discussing the content, they decide on meaningful revisions and make changes directly on the paper. Once students have had ample time (typically five to ten minutes, since these are short paragraphs), we come back together as a class to share our ideas. Volunteers stand and read aloud, incorporating the changes made. Then, we provide feedback. I close the activity by summarizing the weak elements in the piece, restating positive revisions students shared, and concisely listing what a good writer might consider when revising the piece. We may also reread the paragraph as it was first written, then reread one or two revised examples to emphasize how the piece went from "weak" to "good," or even "strong."

Give students practice revising exactly what they need! All you need to do to prepare is to write a paragraph containing weak elements you see in students' writing samples. Compose in the genres and content you're studying. Here's some really good news: Students tend to need the same Peer Revision experiences from year to year. So, once you create a paragraph (or more) for a particular issue, you're bound to use it for many years to come. To get a better handle on this, refer to the list of weak elements (on page 57) and the sample paragraphs that follow (see page 59).

For one of our Peer Revision activities early in the school year, I gave my second graders copies of the following paragraph. Note how short the paragraph is, thus making the assignment very "doable!" (One way I get "buy-in" is to tell the class a student from another year wrote the piece. They love to think they're influencing a peer's writing.)

Spring

I like spring. It is nice. Spring is very, very nice. I like to rollerblade outside. The weather is nice. I like spring.

Students worked to revise this paragraph with a partner. After a few minutes, I called on volunteers to share. Here are some examples of revisions made, along with the feedback I gave.

Jake and Shawn:

Spring

Spring is a blast! I like to go outdoors to rollerblade and play in the park. Spring weather changes all the time. It's great to get outside after a long winter. I love spring!

Thanks for sharing, boys. First, I love how you changed the first line to "Spring is a blast!" This immediately gets my attention and is much more powerful than the dull, voiceless "I like spring." I see you added another activity you like to do in the spring besides rollerblading. This gives the reader more information than just a single example. Good for you! Instead of just saying, "The weather is nice," you were more specific, saying, "Spring weather changes all the time." And, rather than using the worn-out word nice *over and over, you said, "It's great to get outside after a long winter." Class, they did a super job, don't you think? They made the piece stronger by creating a more powerful first sentence, including another springtime activity, and finding alternatives for repeating the word* nice *over and over. Who else would like to share?*

Tamera and Cate:

Spring

I love spring. It is sunny and warm. The beautiful flowers start to bloom. I like to say it's flowerful! Rollerblading around the neighborhood is lots of fun. I love spring!

Thanks! You've made the piece stronger by changing the worn-out, overused word nice *to sunny and warm. This is much more specific. Anything can be nice, but the words "sunny and warm"*

Common Weak Elements for Elementary Writers

- Three-sentence "stories" (especially as you begin the school year)
- "I" pieces (every sentence begins with "I")
- Paragraphs in which almost every sentence starts with "And . . ."
- Incomplete ideas (holes in the content, leaving readers with many questions or confusions)
- Run-on sentences
- Paragraphs that go off topic
- Paragraphs that repeat ideas or sentences
- Paragraphs or stories with no ending or cop-out endings (for example, "She woke up. It was a dream." Or, "To be continued . . .")
- Paragraphs with worn-out descriptors ("It was very, very nice.")
- Paragraphs with overused words or that repeat the same word(s) ("She said . . . She said . . . She said . . .")
- Unorganized paragraphs (both fiction and nonfiction)
- Dull writing that lacks detail and/or voice
- Grammar issues that usually would be characterized as "editing" issues, though they can be addressed using the Peer Revision technique (subject-verb agreement, past-tense errors, sentence fragments, pronoun errors, illogical verb-tense shifts)

describe the spring. I love your next two lines. Again, you are showing what makes spring nice instead of just saying, "It is nice." You say, "The beautiful flowers start to bloom. I like to say it's flowerful!" I love how you made up your own word here. It adds voice to the piece. Also, the detail of rollerblading "around the neighborhood" is more specific than "outside." Great job, girls. Would anyone else like to comment or share?

After a few more examples are shared, I close the lesson.

Ms. Wag: *What made the paragraph I handed out weak?*

Ryan: *It repeated the same old worn-out words over and over.*

Calli: *It was boring!*

Kyle: *There weren't any power words to make the writing more interesting.*

Jace: *It didn't have details.*

Ms. Wag: *Yes! These are all things that made the paragraph weak. But good writers know they can always make revisions to strengthen a piece. The examples shared included these positive changes: making the lead sen-*

tence stronger and more interesting, using alternative words for the worn-out words very *and* nice, *adding describing words like* sunny *and* flowerful, *and adding specific details like rollerblading around the neighborhood and that the weather changes all the time. These are revision strategies you can use anytime to make your writing stronger. Now that you have your revision eyes on, let's start Writing Workshop by rereading a page of your own writing. Can you strengthen the page? Can you write better leads? Can you add details or be more specific? Are there any worn-out or lifeless words you can change? Do you repeat or overuse certain words? If you can, make some revisions, then find someone to share them with!*

One of the absolute pleasures of Peer Revision is seeing students enjoy the process (Enjoy revision? Yes, they can!) and experience success. I've been lucky enough to have some of my work with writers recorded and used for teacher-training purposes.* When I use the clips in workshops, I always get a kick out of the one on Peer Revision. It is a hoot to view students' seriousness and enthusiasm. After cooperatively deciding on a change, one boy smiles at his comrade, shakes his head, and exclaims, "Oh, yeah. That's . . . that's good!"

Hint for Success

When volunteers share their examples, walk over to their desks so you can see their writing. This way, when you comment for the class, you can quickly and easily repeat their words and make specific comments without taxing your memory.

Reminders

✦ Start by modeling the Peer Revision process using the overhead or document camera. (See sample paragraphs, page 59.) Think aloud while making changes to the paragraph(s). Students need to see how to revise. (Modeled Writing provides this type of reinforcement, too.)

✦ Then, do some examples *together* as a class. Shared and guided experiences will help students build the skills they need to be successful with a peer during peer revision exercises and when they're revising their own writing.

✦ Provide many opportunities to engage in Peer Revision—don't just try it a few times and stop.

✦ Repeat lessons when necessary. (For example, if you do a Peer Revision paragraph in October with the word *and* starting every sentence, repeat the lesson in a different paragraph in December, February, and so on as students demonstrate the need in their writing.)

✦ Tie conferences back to Peer Revision activities. When you see a student writing with a weak element you've already studied, remind her of the Peer Revision experience: "Remember, during one

---

*You can preview the video training programs "Enhancing Students' Growth as Writers, Part I and II" at www.ber.org.

Sample Paragraphs for Peer Revision Activities

Recess

Recess is fun. It is my favorite time at school. I play many games with my friends.

Camping

I like to go camping with my family. And we have a big camper. And when we get there, we set up tents. And we cook outside. Camping with my family is fun.

Spiders

Spiders are not insects. Many people are afraid of spiders. Few spiders are poisonous. Spiders have eight legs. There are types of spiders with no eyes at all and others with many eyes. Spiders have two main body parts. They live in many places. They build many different kinds of webs.

Animal Habitats

Animals live in many different habitats. Some live in oceans. Lizards need warmth because they are cold-blooded. The desert makes a nice home for them. Ocean dwellers eat the plants and animals that live in the ocean. Animals live in either water habitats like ponds and oceans, or land habitats like deserts and forests.

Outdoor Classrooms

Every school should definitely have outdoor classroom areas. These areas can be used to study things that are hard to study indoors. They can also be used to do experiments. Kids are more interested when they can study something real and they can study outdoors. To get money, we can have a fundraiser.

of our Peer Revision activities, we practiced making the writing stronger by making sure every sentence doesn't start with *and*? We crossed out the *and*s and simply started with the next word. So, what might you try?"

◆ Tie celebrations back to Peer Revision experiences: "I see Julio made some revisions. Look how he crossed out this *and* and started his sentence with the next word instead. We practiced this technique in a Peer Revision activity, remember?"

JUST ASK IT!

This idea combines a thoughtful responding technique with a great way to spur meaningful revision. When students listen to one another's writing, if a question pops into their heads, I teach them to "Just Ask It!" The idea here is not to evaluate the question, but to ask it right away so the author may consider it. The author can then choose to make a notation in his text so he can come back and elaborate or clarify content later. Once students learn the basics of responding, I get the Just Ask It! technique started through shared experiences.

Ms. Wag: *Boys and girls, we're going to try a new responding technique today designed to help you spot holes in the content of your writing. Holes in your content happen when you haven't explained or shown something fully or clearly enough and you end up leaving your reader with lots of questions. Here's how it works. Santos agreed to share his writing with you. As he reads, if a question pops into your head, I want you to Just Ask It! Raise your hand and he'll call on you. Once the question is asked, Santos can consider it and make a notation to remind himself to come back to it to revise. Let's try it together. You'll see how this technique can be very helpful!*

Santos: [Begins reading his piece] *We're planning a trip to Silver Lake. We'll be going out on the water in a small boat.* [Students raise their hands, Santos calls on one.]

Sheila: *Who's the we?*

Santos: *Oh, my family——my dad, my brother, and me.*

Ms. Wag: *Great! You can make a note like just jotting "who?" here* [pointing in Santos's writing] *or make a revision right now to clarify who you're talking about.* [Santos crosses a single line through "We're" and writes "My family" above it. A few students still have hands up. Santos calls on another.]

Chris: *What kind of boat are you going on?*

Santos: *We have to rent a boat—just a little rowboat.*

Ms. Wag: *So, you could add a detail about that if you wish. Do you want to make a note?*

Santos: *Well, I didn't say anything about getting the boat, but later I talk about rowing it.*

Ms. Wag: *Hmmm, you could make a quick note and decide later if something needs to change.*

Santos: *Okay.* [He writes "kind?" above the word *boat*, then continues reading] *We're going to go fishing so we'll bring all our gear.* [Students raise hands; Santos calls on one.]

Jordan: *What kind of gear do you take?*

Santos: *Well, fishing poles, bait, life jackets, lunch, hats . . . lots of stuff.*

Ms. Wag: *Hmmm, what do you think? Do you want to make a note or change here?*

Santos: *I don't know.*

Ms. Wag: *When I'm not sure, I just make a note so I can remember what was asked and consider further, on one of my rereads, if I need to make a change or add anything.* [Santos jots "poles, bait" . . . above the word *gear*. He reads on.]

Santos: *My favorite part of these fishing trips is the excitement when a fish bites on a line! I love to reel them in!* [Hands go up, Santos calls on a volunteer.]

Nathan: *What kind of fish do you catch there?*

Santos: *Oh, I talk about that later. Usually trout, and we eat them for dinner.*

Ms. Wag: *That's an excellent question, Nathan. And, it's great to hear you include that detail in your writing, Santos. So, you don't need to jot anything there.* [Santos continues reading and the class continues asking questions.]

Kids are natural questioners, so this strategy comes easily to them. Notice how many reasonable questions were asked in just a few lines of text! This demonstrates how extremely useful their input can be, which further motivates thoughtful response. It also reinforces that they are in control of their writing—they must evaluate questions or responses to decide if the questions or responses have merit and whether or not to clarify or elaborate. What a great use of higher-level thinking skills!

Common Question

"When do you use the Just Ask It! technique?"

I teach this technique after students have the basics of thoughtful responding down (see page 26). Once we've practiced together several times, as with Santos's example above, I'll ask students to employ this technique with their triad buddies, particularly when we are working on a class assignment or important project. This can occur during your regular writing workshop time or, if the subject matter falls into a content area, during that content area study time. If desired, you can also teach students to use their Think Pads to jot down questions while an author shares, so they can ask them when he's finished reading.

TELL ME MORE

Another fail-safe way to promote revision is to point to an obvious place in a student's piece and say, "Tell me more." Listen as the child elaborates aloud. Then remark, "Wow, that's interesting. If you include that in your piece, it will make your writing stronger." If the student is reluctant or at a lower skill level, you might record what she said or share the pen with her (interactive writing) to write it down. Otherwise, you can show her how to make an arrow or asterisk to find space elsewhere on the page to write.

> ### Recording Text for your Most Reluctant Writers
>
> With your most reluctant writers, it's fine to occasionally assist by actually recording some or all of what they added aloud. Show them that their talk and their ideas have value. This scaffolding can be a substantial ego-boost, especially when peers give them accolades for their expanded content!

Here's another strategy I use frequently, especially when a student has a very short piece of writing: She reads a sentence (or a few sentences, depending on the length of the work). I say, "Tell me more," listen to her response, then cut the sentence(s) free from the rest of the page and tape them to the top of a new piece of paper. Then I say, "Write down what you just told me here." You can have the student stop and record immediately or continue reading from her original work until you say again, "Tell me more." Listen to her response, cut the section just read from the rest of the piece and tape it to the top of a new page, saying, "Write that here." Carry on until you've worked through all the student has written or until you've met your intended goal. It's amazing how you can assist students in expanding their writing with just scissors, tape, and additional sheets of paper!

Tell me more!

Circling Skills We Know: Successfully Tackling Skill Use in Everyday Writing

Teachers complain about this problem all the time: "Why don't students use the skills they know in their writing? I teach skills explicitly. We practice, they pass the tests, but they still don't apply the skills in their everyday writing. It's so discouraging!" Part of the conundrum is that it's much easier to apply a skill, like capitalizing the first word in a sentence, when that's all students have to worry about (as in completing isolated skill exercises). But the act of writing involves lots of complex brainwork, with a host of skills and strategies at work in tandem. Thus, skill use must be taught and practiced in context—during the real act of writing—so it becomes automatic and habitual. When we see students using skills routinely in their everyday writing, we know they've truly mastered them. This is a step well beyond getting 100 percent on isolated skills tests.

So, how do we achieve this level of proficiency? First, since there's so much involved in composing, we need a method for bringing skill use into focus. I used to do the typical: After students had written something, I'd say, "Did you fix your mistakes?" They often replied, "Oh, yes!" But, in fact, they hadn't even bothered to look back to see if they had made any, and their pieces were commonly error-ridden!

Now, instead of asking them to fix what they did *wrong*, I ask them to look for things they did *right*. We call this Circling Skills We Know. This is a motivating way, rather than a disheartening way, to bring skill use to the forefront.

I introduce Circling Skills* We Know using a piece of my own writing shown on the overhead or document camera, saying, for example,

> *Here is a piece I've been working on about the time I saved the snail from our classroom tank. I've already tried to do my best work as I've written, but I want to step back and reread, with the exclusive purpose of finding skills I've used correctly in my writing. Look! I see I've used capitals for the title [circling the capitals]. I started with a short sentence: "Oh, no!" I used a capital to start the sentence and an exclamation mark at the end [circling both]. Oops! I made a mistake here. I forgot to capitalize the first word in the next sentence. I'll fix that and circle it! Look at all the skills I've already found!*

I continue to review my piece for a few more minutes, circling skills I know, especially those already explicitly covered in class.

Naturally, you'll need to model the strategy in subsequent mini-lessons before most students will be able to apply it. Reinforce your modeling by asking student volunteers to come forward to Circle Skills They

---

*Note: "Skills" refers to writing conventions, mechanics, grammar, and the spelling of high-frequency words, though you may expand how you use this strategy, if you choose (see Common Questions on page 66).

Know with a piece of their own writing in front of the class under your guidance. Another idea is to project student samples (once writers have agreed to this, of course) and invite the class to practice Circling Skills We Know together.

Once students have had plenty of exposure to the strategy, ask them to practice Circling Skills We Know regularly. For example, once a week you might say, "As we begin our workshop today, let's take five minutes to review a piece you're currently working on. Go back and reread at least one page of your writing for Circling Skills We Know. Then, you'll meet briefly with your Triad Buddies (see page 80) to examine your circles." Students really enjoy showcasing what they know! Logically, your next step would be to celebrate students who are doing this well by sharing their samples on the overhead or with the document camera.

As you can imagine, when students go back to circle what they've done correctly, they find mistakes. So, they fix them and circle them, too! (See figure below.) Include this strategy in your modeling and instruction and celebrate when you see this as well.

In addition to regularly requiring students to review their work, circle their skills, and check with a peer(s), ask them to Circle Skills We Know when they are given an assignment headed for publishing or when they choose to publish something they've written on their own. They should complete their review and circling before they put their name on the Sign-Up Board to conference (see page 81).

Before putting this routine in place, you may support it by writing a Morning Message to your class each day. I love writing my students a message, regardless of the grade level. It's another form of Modeled Writing and a meaningful way to start the day. We read the message and talk about the day, then I ask students to come forward and Circle Skills We Know. Once I begin asking them to do this in their own writing, they have a firm base already established from our shared experiences.

As additional support, some teachers like to keep a running class list of skills they've covered. Either this is posted or each student has a copy in their writing folder. Then, when they're asked to circle skills, they can refer to their list as a guide. I've

Note how C. J. crossed out the capital *M* in the middle of the third sentence, fixed it with a lowercase *m*, and circled it. Presto . . . editing without pain! Plus, look at how proficient he is in self-monitoring the many skills he's used correctly! Now, that's mastery!

had success using a special word wall called our Help Wall. We cooperatively agree on references for the skills we've studied and post them on the wall. We refer to the wall during modeled and shared writing experiences and students can use it as they circle skills they know. If you'd like to know more about this word wall, see my book *Teaching Reading and Writing With Word Walls* (1999).

If you include Circling Skills We Know in your teaching routine, I guarantee you will be astounded by the difference it makes in your students' skill use in everyday writing! I started trying this technique years ago out of sheer frustration, and it has never failed to produce amazing results!

Common Questions

"When do you begin asking students to Circle Skills They Know?"

Since this is a long-term goal, and our efforts must focus on meeting short-term goals first, I usually don't begin working in these mini-lessons until about six weeks into the school year. At that time, we typically start easing into official conferences, too.

"I like this strategy, but in the end, how often do students formally edit?"

Remember, I shared how, when I began teaching writing, I asked students to publish almost everything? That meant we edited almost everything. It was a scramble to keep up and I took a lot of writing home to edit, even with the assistance of adult volunteers. Nowadays, since I realize the folly of that approach and we write much, much more than we could ever possibly review, revise, edit, or publish, I pick and choose when we *formally* apply editing. As mentioned in the Quick-Start Tips (see page 9), you might have students edit parts of pieces or review their work looking for a few focus skill areas, but that doesn't mean you must have them edit everything in a piece or, in fact, do anything more with it. In essence, then, they're doing some formal work on some pieces, but not on every piece. Again, when students choose or are assigned to publish, which we do with much less frequency than other writing, we go through the whole process. This always begins by having students Circle Skills They Know before a formal review or conference.

Writing "Band-Aids"

When students type or re-write a piece during publishing, little mistakes still occur, even though they're working from an edited copy. If the piece was done on a computer, it's easy to fix as long as they've been taught to save their work. However, when mistakes happen in rewritten work, use one of these quick fixes: 1) cut a white computer label to fit over the error and correct it; or 2) if the error is more extensive, use Post-it® tape to cover it. These "writing band-aids" can be real lifesavers!

Also, in general, let your students' needs and goals lead you. You might start having them circle skills more often at first and, as you observe they are regularly successful using the skills you've taught in their everyday writing, you can back off. Likewise, if a student is not doing her best, I will ask her to meet with me in conference and we'll set individual goals. For instance, if her work is not up to par in her use of conventions, if she's being careless or sloppy, I may require her to circle skills she knows and meet with me for a quick check more often than I require of other students until her skill levels improve. (For more, see Chapter 7, Classroom Management and Student Accountability.)

"Can I have students circle other things they know in their writing?"
Yes. You might have students review their writing and circle examples of your focus objectives. You should alert them ahead of time, though, so they can put forth extra effort to include them in their writing. Research shows achievement goes up when a clear target is identified. For instance, if you're studying how authors craft descriptive language, have worked on it in Modeled Writing, have practiced with Quick Tries, and are collecting samples in your Quality Writing Notebook (see page 78), you might have students complete a Quick Write with a special focus on using descriptive language. Then, they can go back and circle descriptive parts in their pieces and share with a peer.

One note of caution: If your students' use of mechanics, conventions, and grammar is way below grade-level expectations, you may want to reserve the circling strategy for that focus. Imagine having students circling all kinds of things all the time. The strategy would lose its power. Again, then, let your students' needs be your guide.

What About Spelling?

In daily writing, all students come across words they don't know how to spell. Traditional spelling lists and tests don't help them develop strategies for tackling these unknown words. Students must develop such strategies to reach their full potential as writers. Currently, I work as a literacy coach in a Title I school filled with struggling students. When I first brought up writing with the faculty, the first question I received was: "How are we supposed to write throughout the day and have Writing Workshop? My kids can't spell and they can't even put together a decent sentence." This was from a fifth-grade teacher. Her sentiments resonate with a great number of teachers across grade levels nationwide. Some report not writing as much as they'd like because they are frustrated by

> **"Students who struggle mightily with spelling or worry unnecessarily about perfect spelling do not write fluently or easily."**
>
> —Templeton (2003)

students' constant appeals, "How do you spell . . . ? How do you spell . . . ? How do you spell . . . ?" It is true; students who lack spelling skills and confidence consistently struggle, and many even avoid writing. At the very least, many resort to using easier words, the ones they know how to spell, rather than using more powerful words.

Of course, one solution to this problem is to have students writing from day one in kindergarten. Then, as they grow, writing is a natural part of what they do, and with good instruction, spelling isn't an issue (Wagstaff, 1997, 1999, 2009).

CHALLENGE WORDS

In your own classroom, today, right now, think about how you "teach" spelling strategies. What do you do when asked, "How do you spell . . . ?" Most commonly, students are simply encouraged to spell words "the way they sound" in their everyday writing. However, they are rarely provided guided practice in what that means. Without it, their spelling attempts are haphazard. I found this to be true early on in my teaching—I frequently was unable to read my students' writing because of spelling issues (in particular, I couldn't figure out the words they invented by sounding them out). So, I developed Challenge Words lessons. The goal of these experiences is to provide guided practice in the steps good spellers use to come up with spellings for words they don't know. In a nutshell, the lessons build students' skill and confidence in spelling independently.

I open the lesson by asking students to volunteer some challenging words, ones tough enough to force us to think and use our spelling strategies: "We all come to words we're not sure how to spell when we write. We have to know strategies for getting these words down on paper. We need to feel comfortable giving these types of words a good try, otherwise it makes writing very difficult. That's why we do Challenge Words lessons. They're like warm-ups for writing, since the same steps we practice together will help you when you spell on your own. So, who has a challenging word they've worked on recently in their writing?"

We take about seven to ten minutes to work through two or three words. (When you're just beginning Challenge Words lessons with your class, you may have to suggest words until they get the idea.) Let's look at an example: A student volunteers *outrageous,* and I follow with, "Yes, *outrageous* is a challenging word. I'm glad you offered this word since it could be a powerful one to use in

Chunks

Chunks are often called "spelling patterns" or "rimes." If you're unfamiliar with these terms, here's a definition: A chunk is the part of a syllable that includes the vowel and any letters that follow. So, *ick* is the first chunk in the word *sticky,* while *y* is the second chunk; in the word *flowering,* the first chunk is *ow,* the second is *er,* and the third is *ing.*

writing—much better than more common words like *crazy* or *unusual*. Okay, boys and girls, let's give it a try . . . *outrageous.* Say the word with me."

Students give the word a Quick Try (see page 31) in their Think Pads. As they spell, I walk around the room looking for different attempts. I give two or three students markers so they can come forward and write their variation on the board. Next, I work with the class to analyze the spellings, syllable by syllable, looking for good, logical risk taking (see sample below). I always emphasize that I've called these volunteers forward not because their spellings are necessarily correct but because they were practicing good spelling strategies.

We process each attempt and give feedback:

✦ Did the student chunk the word (divide the word into syllables)?

✦ Did the student "hear" and represent each chunk?

✦ Is there a vowel in every chunk?

✦ Is each chunk spelled logically? (that is, if the chunk is *ack* as in *attacking*, did the student use *a-c-k* since that is the correct spelling of the chunk as it appears in many other words?)

✦ Does the word look right?

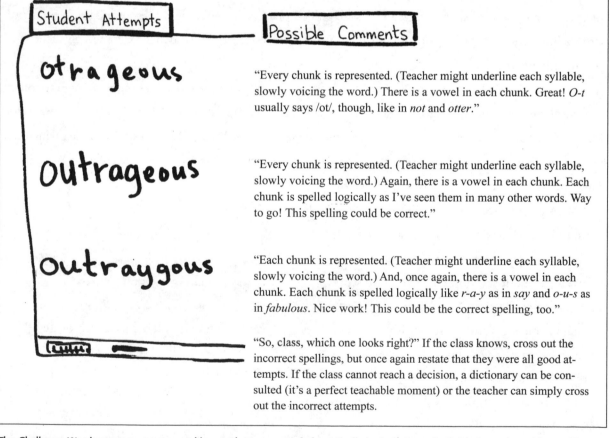

Student Attempts	Possible Comments
otrageous	"Every chunk is represented. (Teacher might underline each syllable, slowly voicing the word.) There is a vowel in each chunk. Great! *O-t* usually says /ot/, though, like in *not* and *otter*."
Outrageous	"Every chunk is represented. (Teacher might underline each syllable, slowly voicing the word.) Again, there is a vowel in each chunk. Each chunk is spelled logically as I've seen them in many other words. Way to go! This spelling could be correct."
Outraygous	"Each chunk is represented. (Teacher might underline each syllable, slowly voicing the word.) And, once again, there is a vowel in each chunk. Each chunk is spelled logically like *r-a-y* as in *say* and *o-u-s* as in *fabulous*. Nice work! This could be the correct spelling, too."
	"So, class, which one looks right?" If the class knows, cross out the incorrect spellings, but once again restate that they were all good attempts. If the class cannot reach a decision, a dictionary can be consulted (it's a perfect teachable moment) or the teacher can simply cross out the incorrect attempts.

The Challenge Words strategy stresses making students aware of phonetically logical attempts. Guided practice with specific feedback increases their ability to represent words logically, which translates into spelling growth.

Afterward, I ask students to review their own attempt, cross out the incorrect parts, then end by writing the correct spelling in their Think Pads.

Once your students have had many Challenge Words lessons, these good spelling strategies become habits. Through this concrete practice, they learn to listen for the chunks in words and to use the spellings of words or word parts they know to more logically spell words or word parts they're struggling with. They gain confidence and are much more willing and able to take risks with spelling, even with larger, multisyllabic words (Wagstaff, 1994, 1999, 2009).

Note: If your students are not comfortable coming forward to write their attempts in front of the class, simply have them call out their spellings while you write a few on the board or overhead. Then proceed to analyze each attempt. This is especially important as you begin the school year since students are just learning about the safety of the environment and about taking risks. They need to gain trust in the fact you mean what you say about spelling, namely: It doesn't have to be correct, but it should be a good, logical try. Until students really know this and gain useful spelling skills through practice, many will show hesitation in their everyday writing, which will interrupt their fluency.

Closing the Lesson

To conclude Challenge Words lessons, debrief explicitly with the class, "Okay, what did we do as spellers to tackle these challenging words?" List the steps aloud, thereby reviewing what writers do when they come across words they don't know how to spell in anything they're writing. Highlight how proficiency with these strategies increases overall ease in writing and enables writers to use any words they want, not just those they know how to spell.

Common Questions

"What if my students don't come up with logical attempts like those shown above?"

You might handle this problem two ways. First, if your students aren't coming close to the challenge word, the word may be too hard for their skill levels. Use this information to adjust your lesson—give students easier words to try. You might say, "I saw a student try to spell the challenge word *tornado* in his writing. I'd like you to try it, too, so you can practice using your good spelling strategies. Say the word with me: *tornado*." As students gain experience, you can adjust the difficulty of the words to meet their needs. Certainly, Challenge Words lessons can also occur in small-group settings to differentiate.

Another way to boost students' skills with challenge words is to model the thinking processes you want them to use. For example, if the word *spectacular* is volunteered and, as you circulate, you notice this word is much too hard, go to the board, stop the class, and think aloud, working through the word.

You can also model generating a few different, logical attempts, then stepping back to decide which looks best (spellers sometimes use this strategy).

"How often do you do Challenge Words lessons?"

I incorporate Challenge Words lessons into our schedule at least once a week. To jump-start students' skills and confidence at the beginning of the year, it's beneficial to practice more often—two or three times a week. When you work on just two or three words a session, as I recommend, the lessons take less than ten minutes.

Sticky-Note Spelling

All teachers who incorporate writing into their curriculum find students asking, "How do you spell . . . ?" Some students ask incessantly, thus significantly slowing down their fluency. So, how do we provide quick, concrete help without doing all the work (just spelling words for them) or resorting to the overused prompt "Just spell it how it sounds"? Sticky-Note Spelling enables us to effectively guide individuals, capitalizing on the same strategies in our Challenge Words lessons (see previous section). We want to communicate, "Help is available, but the work won't be done for you." After all, students need to become independent problem solvers.

Sticky note with analogous words to help student write the word *stupidly*.

I keep pads of sticky notes around the room. When a student asks how to spell a word, I first prompt her with the strategies we're practicing in Challenge Words lessons: Say it, chunk it, think of other words you know with those chunks. Sometimes this is all the support that's needed. If the student is able to come up with analogous words for the chunks in the unknown word, I ask her how to spell them. If she can, she writes them on a sticky note and takes it to her desk to help spell the new word. If not, I spell the analogous words for her, give her the note, and send her on her way to generate the spelling independently. If she cannot give me any words that sound the same or have the same chunks, I assist her in hearing the word parts, then provide analogous words on the sticky note, as below.

KENDRA: *How do you spell* stupidly?

Ms. WAG: *What are the chunks you hear in* stupidly?

KENDRA: *I don't know.*

Ms. WAG: *Let's clap the chunks:* stu pid ly. *Do you know any other words with any of those same chunks?*

KENDRA: *No.*

Ms. Wag: *Okay, well, I know* flu, *which sounds like* stu, *and is spelled the same.* [I write the word *flu* on the sticky note, underlining *u*.] *I know how to spell* kid, *which sounds like* pid. [I write the word *kid* on the sticky note, underlining *id*]. *And, look on our Word Wall! The word* slowly *has* ly *at the end just like* stupidly. [I write the word *slowly* on the sticky note, underlining *ly*.] *Now, use these words to spell* stupidly *in your writing.*

You don't need a word wall to use this technique. If you have one and can make connections to words on the wall, be sure to do so! This demonstrates real use of the word wall, which should be your goal. If you don't have one, or an analogous word is not available on your wall, simply provide words from memory.

Variation on Sticky-Note Spelling

When a student asks for spelling help, write two words on the sticky note (one analogous and one not analogous) for each chunk in the unknown word. This way, the student must discern which is helpful (see example at right).

Sticky note with analogous words to help student write the word *fabulous*

Mario: *How do you spell* fabulous?

Ms. Wag: *What's the first chunk you hear in* fabulous?

Mario: *I don't know.*

Ms. Wag: *Let's break it down together. Clap with me:* fab u lous. *Here are two words* [writing *pop* and *tab* on the sticky note]. *Read them with me.*

Mario and Ms. Wag: Pop. Tab.

Ms. Wag: *Which one sounds the same as the first chunk of* fabulous?

Mario: Tab.

Ms. Wag: *That's right!* Tab *sounds like* fab *and has the same spelling pattern. You can use the chunk in* tab *to spell* fab [underlining *ab* and crossing out the word *pop* on the sticky note]. *What's the next chunk you hear?*

Mario: U.

Ms. Wag: *How do you think that part is spelled?*

Mario: *Probably with a* u.

Ms. Wag: *Yep!* [writing the letter *u* on the sticky note] *Now, which of these words will help you spell the last chunk?* [writing *marvelous* and *probably* on the sticky note] *Read them with me.*

Mario and Ms. Wag: *Marvelous. Probably.*

Mario: *I don't know.*

Ms. Wag: *Say* fabulous *with me. Now, say* marvelous *and* probably. *Which sounds the same at the end?*

Mario: Marvelous.

Ms. Wag: *Yes!* [underlining *ous* and crossing out *probably*] *The last chunk in the word* marvelous *is spelled the same as the last chunk in the word* fabulous. *You have all the help you need.* [hands Mario the sticky note to take to his desk]

Looking back on this dialogue, it seems like a long process. It really is not. Often, students can point out the analogous word for some of the chunks, just not all of them. If you find a student cannot decide which word is helpful, even after rereading them and repeating the word he's trying to spell, just cross out the unhelpful word and move on.

Common Questions

"What if we're doing a Quick Jot or other three-minute writing and a student asks how to spell something? How do you provide spelling support even more quickly than with the sticky notes?"

Naturally, there are times when a student asks for help and you only have a couple of seconds to provide it. You might say, "Remember all the strategies we practice in our Challenge Words lessons? Use what you know: Say the word, chunk it, and think of other words you know with those word parts. Give it your best try." Or, you might take a couple of seconds to model and think aloud on the board: "Let's see. The word is *factory*? Hmmm, if I chunk it, I hear, fac / tor / y [*writing three horizontal lines to indicate syllables*]. Well, I know /f/ and /act/—a-c-t [*writing* f-a-c-t *on the board*], then I hear /or/—lots of kids would just put the letter *r* here, but I know that syllable must have a vowel. /Or/ is spelled just like the word *or*, so it's o-r [*writing* o-r *on the board*]. Lastly, I know *Mary*—her name ends in *y*, which sounds like /ee/ like in *factory*. So, I need a *y* [*writing* y *on the board*], and *y* acts as a vowel in the last syllable." (Remember to model making connections to your word walls if you have them.) This quick modeling is reinforcing to everyone in the class, but don't overuse it. You don't want to communicate that you'll frequently do all the work for students.

"What about struggling spellers in upper grades?"

As upper-elementary-grade teachers, we all have students who need the practice of Challenge Words and the support of Sticky-Note Spelling. Even when 90 percent of the students are proficient spellers, that leaves 10 percent who need this type of instruction to gain access to the world of writing. Don't forget that 10 percent! These lessons are perfectly suited to their needs and can be done in advance of the study of roots, morphemes, and derivations. Teaching the strategy of making analogies works with these word parts, as well.

"Are you advocating incorrect spelling in many of these lessons?"

I much prefer taking an active role in my students' spelling growth to giving them lists of words to memorize. Research shows students benefit from learning spelling strategies and having plenty of opportunities to write with feedback so they can hone their skills. When I began teaching, I assigned a spelling list on Monday, had students practice throughout the week, and tested on Friday. I didn't find this method efficacious in improving overall spelling abilities in everyday writing. Words were often learned just for Friday and frequently misspelled the rest of the year. I would much rather skillfully teach what good spellers do and give lots of opportunity to practice, practice, practice with scaffolding, guidance, and feedback.

"But what if I'm required to use the school's or district's spelling program consisting of lists and the usual Monday–Friday cycle?"

You can have students add their Very Own Words to the required lists. Here's a simple way to manage that. Students keep a spiral notebook (we call them Spelling Logs) to list words they misspell in their everyday writing. When such a word is recognized during their own rereading of their work, peer review, Circling Skills We Know, editing, conferencing, publishing, or when I'm circulating around the room, they simply list the word in their log. On Monday, invite students to add some of their Very Own Words to their lists. They write their list in their daily planners. You can differentiate and decide who would benefit from doing this and how many words they should add (if you give a pre-test on Monday, you may find some students who already know all the words on the required list). Students indicate when a word has been added to their spelling list by placing a check mark next to it in their log. Then, they practice their words, as usual, during the week. On Friday, after you've read aloud the required spelling list, have the class turn over their test paper and list their Very Own Words. Most students will remember them, but if they need help, a peer can read these words from the daily planner. Voilá! Individualized spelling made easy!

"Are these the only lessons you use to teach spelling?"

No. We haven't touched on irregular high-frequency words such as *come, said,* and *they* except to mention these words during Circling Skills We Know. No matter what grade I'm teaching, we have a small word wall, called the Words We Know Wall, to effectively address these and support students in spelling them correctly in their everyday writing. If you find your students experience difficulty with such words, you might refer to my book *Teaching Reading and Writing With Word Walls* (Scholastic, 1999).

Evaluating Spelling

Teachers often use developmental continuums or spelling stages to evaluate students' spelling in process writing and to guide their instruction. These approaches yield data that is much more useful in really understanding how students are growing as spellers than do traditional list-tests. After all, how students spell in their everyday writing is truly where the rubber hits the road in terms of their spelling abilities.

Here's a quick way to get reliable data from students' writing samples:

- ✦ Count the total number of words in a completed piece
- ✦ Count the number of words spelled conventionally in the piece
- ✦ Divide the number of words spelled conventionally by the total number of words to calculate the percentage correct

Doing this just three times a year can be a real eye-opener. Plus, you can use the total number of words written as an indication of growth in writing fluency over time!

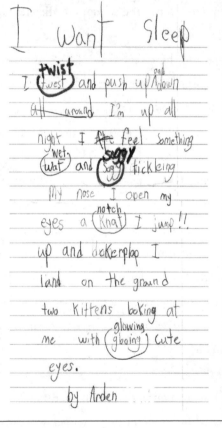

A second grader's baseline sample from August. Total number of words: 25. Nine are spelled correctly, equaling a 36% conventional spelling rate. The poem is titled "The Butterfly" and reads "The butterfly / is so colorful. / I wish / it would / come to / me. Oh wow! / It landed / on my hand. / Come back / butterfly."

A May sample from the same second grader. Total number of words: 50, with 45 spelled correctly, equaling a 90 percent conventional spelling rate! This represents tremendous spelling growth and much improved ease and fluency with writing. Her other spring samples mirror this effect. That's the power of writing every day coupled with targeted instruction! The poem is titled "I Want Sleep" and reads "I twist and push up and down / I'm up all / night. I feel something / wet and soggy tickling / my nose. I open my / eyes a notch. I jump!! / up and kerplop I / land on the ground / two kittens looking at / me with glowing cute / eyes."

Add-on Writing

Add-on Writing augments the practical revision strategies students learn through Modeled Writing. I developed the technique to give them guided practice targeting revision. Reading a favorite book, completing a content area or genre study, or sharing an experience as a class can be fodder for Add-on Writing. To start off, we generate a related topic, title, and a beginning (typically just two or three sentences). I write the title on the Add-on Writing chart (an easel pad of paper) and invite students to add to the piece. Children come forward any time other than during a lesson and add their ideas (typically a sentence or two) in random order. This naturally creates a need to work on organizing the piece. After a couple of days of adding time, we read it to evaluate how the writing is coming. We discuss possible directions for the piece and allow more time for children to add.

Try Sentence Strips

Instead of using chart paper, you may provide sentence strips for student contributions. This eliminates the need to cut apart charts.

As the piece proceeds, we discuss possible endings or closings/conclusions (depending on the genre). Once we agree we have enough to create a complete piece, we revise and reorganize. Since students have shared ownership based on their contributions, they are more fully engaged and invested in this process. We cut the sentences apart (see box at right) and work together with a pocket chart to cooperatively put the pieces together in the most logical and effective order. We read and reread, analyze, try different leads, reorder sentences, add transitions, change phrases, work on grammar and spelling, omit redundant ideas, consider variations for the ending—you name it! This is a dynamic way to show how fun it can be to muck around in a text . . . and keep coming back to it day after day to make it its best. It may take several days to get the text to the point where it feels "done." But, in the end, you might be surprised about the quality of the writing you produce together! The work will mirror the thinking you do in Modeled Writing, except now you're releasing more responsibility to students. Essentially, they're getting shared, guided practice applying all the skills and strategies we want writers to develop! And, since you're all working together, they still receive a lot of support for success.

Recently, my second graders and I completed a genre study in tall tales (see Modeled Writing to Introduce a New Genre, page 50, for ideas). We decided to write a cooperative tall tale about our class in an Add-on Writing format. We talked about the characteristics of tall tales and began coming up with "whoppers," or exaggerations, about our class. We skipped the title, as students jumped excitedly to generating ideas. I had them share their ideas with a neighbor, then raise their hands to begin the story. The first student volunteered, "The Wag's Winners can tell time as fast as speeding bullets." I recorded this idea and the next from a second volunteer, "They eat lunch in 20 seconds flat!" We reread the two sentences and talked about how we were off to a good start. Next, I reminded everyone they could add to the chart in their free time. After setting the chart aside, there was a flurry of activity throughout the day as students made more contributions.

We reread our story the following day. Several issues popped up and we worked to make a few quick revisions (again, as part of the routine process of rereading while drafting). We determined we needed more content to have a complete story, so additional time was granted.

Here are the actual issues we worked on during that first reading:

✦ **Making the Subject Consistent Throughout** Some students wrote "We" while others wrote "Our class" as they began their sentences. We reread our first two volunteers' contributions, noting how they began as "The Wag's Winners" and "They." Of course, maintaining parallel subject matter references is a common issue, and here, through Add-on Writing, it was reviewed in a real and meaningful context. We crossed out "We" and "Our class," replacing them with "The Wag's Winners," "They," or "The Class," depending on which sounded best.

✦ **Figuring Out a Logical Organization for the Piece** We soon realized, upon reading for the first time, the story was "jumping all over the place!" There was a contribution about math, then one about lunch, then one about reading, then one referring to math again, then one on field trips, followed by one about art, and so on. We recognized the need for some kind of plan or outline for how we would organize the ideas. We decided to wait to figure this out until all the student additions had been made.

Two days later, we read the story again. We had four charts full of contributions! As we read, the second page had something we determined could make a good ending: "Our class (we crossed out "Our" and changed it to "The") was so smart that they didn't have to go to school!" We jotted a note (the word *end*) next to the sentence to remind us this might make a perfect

Our Add-on story chart after rereading and making minor revisions

Students categorize the Add-on story sentences by subject area.

ending. As we continued to read, we once again remarked how "jumbled" the story seemed, and found additional places to change "We" and "Our class." As we finished reading, we determined we did indeed have enough content to make a good, complete story and I assigned a few helpers to cut the charts into sentences.

While they were cutting, we entertained ideas on how to organize the piece. After many suggestions, we resolved to categorize the sentences by subject area. Then we could have sections (or paragraphs) on math, reading, art, and other subjects. Given this plan, we put the individual sentences in our reading corner and volunteers worked on categorizing them (see photo on page 76).

For the following few days, we read and reread sentences from one category at a time, playing with their organization in a pocket chart. We found redundant ideas, so we agreed to omit some sentences. As this process continued, category by category, we worked on the following revisions:

✦ Adding transitions ("First," "Next," "Finally")

✦ Signaling the reader when a new category of sentences was introduced: ("In math…" "During writing time . . ." "At lunchtime . . .")

✦ Developing an attention-grabbing lead ("The Wag's Winners is the most exciting class in the whole universe! This story shows you why.")

✦ Rethinking our ending, referring back to the idea we marked, then rereading the endings of several tall tales we had studied

✦ Developing an appropriate title

Add-on Writing enables teachers to guide students through focused, in-depth revision while highlighting organizational issues. It's a shared experience; no one has total ownership of the piece, so we can comfortably delve deeply into revision without crushing anyone's writing ego.

Multiple Add-on Writing experiences compound benefits since similar revision and organizational issues resurface again and again. You'll find these are identical to the issues needing attention in students' work: illogical organization, inconsistencies with verb tense and subject references, writing off-topic, repetitive or redundant ideas, lack of adequate content development, few transitions, identical sentence structure, overuse of "worn-out" words, mixed-up or unclear pronoun references, weak leads or thesis statements, poor endings or conclusions, and so on. After students have been involved in the intense modeling, explanation, negotiating, and rereading/rehearsal required to complete an Add-on Writing piece, they have much more clarity about the nature of the writing process and look at their own work with sharper vision.

Here are a few examples of Add-on Writing I've completed with classes. Imagine how these experiences might unfold as students individually contribute sentences to a chart (or on sentence strips), then work hand-in-hand with you to craft a connected piece.

✦ *A Frog's Life Cycle,* based on our scientific study, readings, and observations about our class pet.

What an outstanding way to culminate a unit of study!

✦ *Our Charity Craft Fair,* based on our experience making and selling holiday crafts to benefit the homeless shelter down the street from our school

✦ *When Earth Dreams,* themed on Earth Day principles and based on the book *When Cats Dream* by Dav Pilkey

✦ *The Good Things About Families,* based on the book *The Tenth Good Thing About Barney* by Judith Viorst

Possible Follow-Up

When you're finished, celebrate with a special class read-aloud. You might light a candle or play some music before and after the reading to mark the occasion. You can also publish in book form. Simply type the text and bind it in a pronged folder. Or, depending on the age of the students and the length of the piece, you may want to type just one or two sentences per page and invite them to illustrate. Another great idea is to take digital photos of the steps or experience, when applicable, and use these to illustrate your text. Students love this!

The Quality Writing Notebook

Quality literature is quality writing. As such, books provide models of the elements of good writing we need to teach. Starting on the very first day of school when I read aloud, I introduce the idea of "reading like writers" (Calkins, 1991, 1994). As I read, I pause to examine cases of clever leads, powerful word choice, good use of voice, quality dialogue, vivid descriptions, effective endings, and so on. It's amazing how a few seconds of thinking aloud and/or discussion can lead to changes in students' writing. This is because I read multiple books aloud every day, always looking for opportunities to model "reading like a writer." So students hear examples of particular writing attributes repeatedly across many books from day to day. These momentary events add up over time to a ton of discussion about the qualities of writing. Since this happens regularly, these qualities are always fresh in students' minds.

Ideas for Your Quality Writing Notebook

Create tabs in a notebook for the elements you teach. These might include:

- clever leads
- effective endings
- powerful word choice
- great voice
- vivid descriptions
- poetic language
- quality dialogue
- useful transitions
- persuasive language
- synonyms for overused words

I used to keep charts of the qualities we noticed. Thus, we had charts titled "Examples of Great Leads," "Examples of Effective Endings," "Examples of Vivid Descriptions," and so on. We stopped and discussed elements as we read aloud and added examples to the appropriate chart. The end result was that we were swimming in posters students barely referenced and the process was taking too much time.

Now, our valuable observations go into a spiral notebook titled our "Quality Writing Notebook." I create sections with tabs at the beginning of the year (see sample tab labels in box on previous page), and we record examples as we go. When we encounter something noteworthy, we put a sticky tab on the page of the book and a volunteer later copies the example in the appropriate section of our class reference notebook. This saves time, bolsters students' ownership, and is much more practical than posters.

We use our Quality Writing Notebook to reinforce points made in mini-lessons. Additionally, students refer to the notebook when they need inspiration or are working on a certain trait in their own writing. As the year progresses, we add samples from our very own classroom authors—particularly those noticed by peers!

Over time, with continual talk about the qualities, students start to use the language of good writing. I hear them say, "That's a great lead!" or "That ending really works. Let's add it to our notebook." I hear these spontaneous comments during reading, writing, and sharing times. I love it when a student comes to me during silent reading and says, "Wow! Look at this! What a powerful description. We need to share it with the class and put it in our Quality Writing Notebook!"

Moving on With Student Responding: Sharing Circles and Triad Buddies

Since writers need multiple opportunities to get response, we use Sharing Circles and Triad Buddies. These are simple techniques that build on the responding skills covered in Chapter 2. You'll see, each has different benefits.

SHARING CIRCLES

Sharing Circles are employed during writing workshop. We begin using them only after students have the fundamentals of thoughtful responding under their belts—generally not until several weeks into the workshop. I lean a small whiteboard against a wall, where students can sign up to be part of a responding group. When there are three names on the board, there are enough members for a Sharing Circle. The three find a spot in the room, sit in a tight circle (knee touching knee), share their writing one at a time, and respond to one another's work.

Sometimes I call a Sharing Circle together. If I find, during circulating, conferring, or reviewing work, that students need help, I'll have a circle come together for a particular purpose. This might even be just for editing. During these occasions, I may ask one writer to share and the other two to give a response. Here's an example: Adam, a third grader, labored for almost two weeks to write about his little brother. He had one of Nicholas's characteristics (sometimes accompanied by a funny story or vignette) on each of ten pages, with illustrations. In conference, he announced his desire to bind the pages together into a book. We agreed he needed some kind of closing to tie all of Nicholas's quirky characteristics together. He was completely stuck. I was also at a loss.

To help, I called a Sharing Circle together consisting of two other boys. Adam asked them to listen carefully to his piece and give him suggestions for how he might end it. After just a few minutes, the group bounded up to me proudly and announced, "We've got it!" At right . . . their clever ending.

TRIAD BUDDIES

Related to Sharing Circles are Triad Buddies (adapted from Bureau of Education and Research Video Training Program: Enhancing Students' Growth as Writers). Groups of three are assigned to work together for a term. Anytime a teacher wants to provide extra help and/or response or needs to heighten accountability with review, he may call for the class to meet with their Triad Buddies. The assigned groups quickly get together and work at giving the particular feedback needed. For example, the teacher might say: "We've been focusing on using proper end punctuation. Each triad should look exclusively for the use of periods, question marks, and exclamation points in the assignment. Read at least one page of each writer's piece aloud so you can hear where the stops belong." Or . . . "We've been working on crafting effective dialogue. Thanks for practicing today during our Quick Try. Quickly join your triad buddies, read your Quick Tries aloud, and respond thoughtfully using our rubric for effective dialogue." The triads can meet for a very brief session, as would be the case with these examples, or a longer session, depending on the focus and the needs of the students.

We've covered a great deal of ground in this chapter. If you're just starting out, try one or two techniques at most, and give yourself time to learn and reflect. When you're comfortable, add another technique, using your students' needs to prioritize.

CHAPTER 6

Managing Conferences

Though volumes of admirable work have been produced about effectively conferencing with student writers, my best advice is: Keep it simple. Don't burden yourself thinking you must follow this or that model. Start slow, experiment, and recognize there is no one "right way" to "do" conferences. You can always jump in using a few pointers, then research more about the process once you get your feet wet. Like anything else, concern about doing it "right" should not hold you back from giving it a go.

The Sign-up Board

The first concern teachers often have about holding conferences with writers is how to manage the meetings. We all need an easy system. Here's what I do: I lean a whiteboard against a filing cabinet and students sign up to conference when they:

- ✦ want response or feedback
- ✦ are finished with something and want to publish
- ✦ need help in addition to that provided by peers
- ✦ are asked by the teacher to conference (as when I review work and find a conference is needed with a child or group for a particular purpose, and when we are completing a formal assignment)
- ✦ need to set/review writing goals

This list is not exhaustive. Students may sign up for other reasons, but this is a good base to begin your conversations with the class about why writers confer.

While Writers Wait to Conference

Next, teachers ask: What do students do once they sign up? We all want to avoid management snafus, so it's imperative students have clear direction in what to do so they're using every minute of Open Writing Time productively. Post a list with options and explicitly teach about each. The list I post is titled "While Writers

Wait" and includes:

✦ Work on any pending writing assignment

✦ Begin a new piece of (choice) writing

✦ Review/add to your Running Topics List

✦ Reread pieces in your Think Pad or writing workshop folder

✦ Reread the work of other writers or class collections

✦ Respond to the work of others

✦ Share your writing with a buddy

✦ Sign up for a Sharing Circle

✦ If publishing: Work on presentation, illustrations, book cover, or Author's Page (see box)

Perhaps some of these options will work for your class. Some teachers combine their reading and writing workshops, so when students are "finished" with a piece or are waiting to confer, they work on reading workshop activities.

When Should I Start Holding Conferences?

To start, think "first things first." The work of getting the workshop running smoothly and relatively independently has to be done before you start in-depth, formal conferences. Like any other big routine you're putting into place, you need to go slowly. Think of reading: As I mentioned before, you wouldn't begin pulling small groups for guided reading until the rest of the class knows and adheres to expectations. Don't pressure yourself and your writers into "officially" conferring too early. Remember, after your mini-lesson, it's beneficial to circulate and assist students as needed, holding "mini-conferences" at tables. These may include answering questions, responding to content, publicly commenting about positive aspects in a writer's behavior or piece, redirecting students, and so on. These

Publishing

Students may publish in many ways. Often, they can begin the steps needed for their particular form of publishing (e.g., producing a book) before they meet with the teacher. The ideas listed are just a few examples of what they might do. Sometimes, for example, a student might spend his time practicing his poem aloud to get the proper rhythm and cadence for an oral presentation as he awaits his turn to conference.

Where We Conference

When I began conferring, I called students to a "conferencing table" in the back of the room as I worked down our Sign-Up Board. I noticed it took students a minute to gather their materials and respond to my call, resulting in wasted time. Now, I confer right at students' desks. This is much faster and students seated around us benefit from listening in a bit to the conference. However, if something sensitive needs to be addressed in the conference, we find a private place to meet.

quick interactions help students learn what to do and how to do it while your availability during circulating will allow you to manage any concerns that arise on the spot.

Once you feel students are managing their writing time well, "official" conferences may begin. It might take up to six weeks to get to this point. This is fine since students are getting plenty of response to their writing by working together during Open Writing Time, having teacher interaction as she circulates, and using Everybody Share Time, Author's Chair, and possibly even Sharing Circles and Triad Buddies. Plus, if you engage in quick bursts of writing across the curriculum, students are continually getting responses to their writing. Response is just part of the daily routine.

Conferencing How-Tos

As we begin to reflect on the conferring process, let me share one of my favorite cartoons on the subject. A boy brings his writing to the teacher, who is sitting at her desk. She looks disapprovingly at the piece, stating, "You're handwriting is terrible. You haven't used punctuation and your spelling is atrocious!" The boy looks up at the teacher hopefully and says, "Well, aside from all that, how did you like it?" And . . . there is the big picture in a nutshell! Think how this correlates to the priorities discussed in Setting Short-Term Goals (page 13) and Building Motivation by Celebrating Students' Writing (page 17)!

Since students put their hearts and minds on paper when they write, they naturally want a response to the content first, before they're open to anything else. So, after you ask the student why he signed up for the conference, start there. Have the student read his piece (or part of the piece, if it is particularly long) and respond to the content *only*. Make positive remarks to show you've heard what's being said and that you're interested. Basically, have a brief conversation about what's he's written. Hint: If you've never conferred before, just think of it as having conversations with students about their ideas. If you begin with this in mind, you'll start out on the right foot and you can grow from there.

Next, ask questions. This is natural in conversation and a wonderful bridge to revision. If there is anything in the content that is confusing or needs elaboration, form a question about it. Yes, you might also make suggestions. When possible, tie your comments back to your mini-lessons, Peer Revision Activities (page 55), Quick Writes (page 38), and Add-on Writing (page 74) experiences. Also, ask the writer what he feels could be done to make his piece stronger. You might help him make a few revisions right on the spot.

Then, consider his goals and the nature of the piece. If he's choosing to publish or has been assigned to do so, be sure he's already circled skills he knows (see page 63) to begin the editing process. Proceed to assist in revision and editing, but only part of the piece if it's lengthy, so you're not spending an inordinate amount of time with one student to the neglect of others. The process might be finished by a volunteer (see Volunteer Conferencing Checklists, page 86) or even sent home for help, if applicable.

Always be realistic about revision and editing, keeping your end goal in mind: to encourage writers to continue their journey and to boost their development. We don't want to pound students into the ground on revision or editing. If a student must revise everything he's just said, he may decide to stop writing entirely. Again, when teachers think everything has to be "fixed," they get overwhelmed with too much to do and often say they don't have time for writing. Does this mean you never work through the process with a whole piece? Again, absolutely not . . . but be choosy about which pieces need this much work and make it your goal to write so often and so much that you can't possibly review, correct, or publish it all even if you wanted to! When this is the case, writing becomes "part of everything we do," just like reading, as I've described throughout the book.

When ending the conference, I may quickly review any major points, then ask, "What are you going to do now?" This way, I'm sure students know what they'll do next.

Obviously, one challenge of conferring is continuing to monitor the rest of the class while attending to the student at hand. "Withitness" is important: Keeping an eye on and commenting aloud about classroom happenings lets students know they are always accountable. While a student is making a correction in his piece, for instance, I might look up and comment, "I see three of our writers are meeting in a Sharing Circle. Look how engaged they are! I can tell they're working productively." Meeting with students at their desks also helps since you're always in close proximity to the main action. Another useful technique is to complete a few conferences, then circulate through the whole class again before doing more.

Common Questions

"What if I can't get through all the conferencing steps?"
Start slow. Do what you can—but try to stretch so you'll grow. Don't stress about getting through all the steps, es-

Give Students the Pen

Students should be holding the pen and in control whenever possible. So if a correction is made, the student is the one recording it on his piece. More is learned this way and deeper ownership is retained.

Summary of Possible Conferencing Steps

- Ask: "Why did you sign up to conference?"

- Student reads his piece (or part of it) aloud

- Converse about the content/respond positively to the content

- Ask questions; make suggestions to clarify or elaborate on content (revision)

- Check focus skill areas (if applicable), congratulate him on skills used correctly (especially on occasions when he circles skills he knows), make corrections (again, when applicable)

- Ask: "What will you do now?" (make sure the writer understands next steps)

pecially if you're a novice (see box, page 84). Depending on how much experience you've had, simply meeting with students to briefly converse about their content might be a colossal step.

The following anecdote may help. When I was teaching second grade, a third-grade teacher friend, Natalie, asked me to help her begin a Writing Workshop in her classroom. I took my class into her room for several weeks, teaching the mini-lessons, holding Open Writing Time, circulating and conferring, then closing with sharing. My class and I visited many times throughout the year; I modeled while Natalie shadowed. She was thrilled with the students' work and became comfortable holding the workshop herself. While learning that first year, she was able to confer with students about their content, but didn't formally address revision or editing. However, the following year, she dove in a little deeper—adding a reasonable revision and editing focus. In subsequent years, she reflected and worked toward additional goals. Now, eight years later, though she's still learning, as we all are, she's an expert teacher of writing and her workshop runs very smoothly.

"If you're not editing and correcting everything, don't the parents and administration complain?"
You must communicate your goals well. Be sure to explain your focus and your short- and long-term goals at back-to-school night and in your course disclosure. Share your views and the research behind them with your administration.

If a parent complains, explain that you write so much daily that you can't possibly review it all. Make the connection to how we handle students' reading volume—we can't possibly listen to them read it all, have them do something formal with all they read, or correct all their reading "mistakes." Practice is part of learning, and volume is important. Certainly, though, you should detail your plans to complete pieces with focus skill areas (these will be closely monitored) and to undergo rigorous editing and review when completing major projects during the year.

Lastly, when anyone questions your approach, invite them in to observe and converse with students about their writing. When they see and hear what's happening, they'll develop a deeper understanding and appreciation for your goals and methods. Plus, you can put them to work as volunteers!

"What if a student chooses too many pieces to take through all the steps to publishing?"
I handle this much like I handle any problem that arises. If most of the class is having trouble with something, I address it in a mini-lesson. If it's a few students, I pull them into a small group during conferencing time to develop a plan. When it's an individual, I confer with that student and set goals. In this case, if the student wants to publish everything, we'd have to set limits and criteria to judge when a piece might be eligible for publishing. On the other hand, if a student never chooses to bring his work through publishing, we'd pick one of his pieces and work to reach small goals all the way through to publishing.

Here's a case in point: A former student of mine, who, by the way, wanted to grow up to be an artist *and* a spy, loved coming up with creative titles for stories and beginning to write them. Then, she'd want to revise and edit that bit and spend her Open Writing Time working on elaborate, artistic book covers. Problem was, she didn't want to go much further. I met with her individually, we selected one of her pieces, set goals and deadlines, and produced a book. When she shared it in the Author's Chair, she received rave reviews. This was all she needed. She was on her way! From then forward, she didn't need my intervention to complete a reasonable number of projects.

Volunteer Conferencing Checklists

Another way to keep conferring manageable is to use volunteers. Our volunteers are often parents, high school helpers, or members of the community. If we're working on a formal assignment where all students will complete all steps of the writing process to publish their pieces, I schedule several volunteers to come in at the same time. Otherwise, I may have one extra helper during Open Writing Time. Still, if volunteers visit our classroom at another time of day, I always start them at the Sign-up Board (see page 81) to help me work down the waiting list before enlisting their assistance other ways. They call the next student on the board and use one of the Volunteer Conferencing Checklists to guide them as they work. The intensive individualized attention is a real boost for students.

Included here are two versions of the checklist: The first includes instructions for providing response only; the second includes instructions for responding *and* providing assistance with revision and editing. Use the second version when you need help with the paperwork on those few formal projects. Additionally, if a child has chosen to publish a particularly long piece, you might complete some of the review process yourself, then enlist the help of a volunteer to finish up or even send home the second version of the checklist, asking families to assist.

I prepare several zippered plastic bags ahead of time so I can quickly grab the desired checklist and get help from virtually anyone who shows up at my classroom door (including the principal!). Each kit includes:

✦ a copy of a Volunteer Conferencing Checklist

✦ a compact dictionary

✦ a pen and pencil

I occasionally use volunteers for desktop publishing, as well. For example, we did so when we typed our Quick Writes about life cycles for a class collection. The volunteer types the pieces during class so he can call students back to help, if needed.

Dear Volunteer,

Thanks for helping! You are such an important part of our writing community! Students love having a special one-on-one audience to share their writing. Your positive comments and questions will empower them even more as writers!

Here are the steps you should take when meeting with a student writer.

1st: Have the student read the piece to you.

2nd: Make positive comments, ask questions, or make suggestions. (See the ideas below.)

3rd: Before the child leaves you, ask him what he is going to do next as a writer. Will he add to his writing based on your comments? Will he start a new piece of writing?

4th: Thank the child for his efforts and encourage him to keep working hard as a writer!

I hope you enjoy sharing the students' writing! Thanks again for your help!

Sincerely,

- -

SUGGESTIONS FOR COMMENTS:

I like how you . . .

I see that you . . .

Why did you . . . ?

Tell me more about . . .

I have a question about . . .

Why don't you think about . . . ?

Where might you add more details about . . . ?

I don't understand _____ about . . . .

I like the word you used here because . . .

This is very descriptive . . .

I could picture in my mind how you . . .

Maybe you could . . .

Dear Volunteer,

Thanks for helping! We couldn't do all this important writing work without the support of people like you. Here are the steps you should take when helping a student revise and edit her writing.

1st: Have the student read the piece to you. Comment on the story content (not the grammar, spelling, or anything else yet). Here are some suggestions for comments.

I see you've written about . . .

I like how you . . .   This is very descriptive . . .

I see that you . . .   What a good title . . .

Why did you say . . . ?   Maybe you could . . .

Tell me more about . . .   Why don't you think about . . . ?

I see you used this powerful word . . .

I see you used this powerful sentence . . .

Where might you add more details about . . . ?

I don't understand _____ about . . .

I have a question about . . .

2nd: After making positive comments, asking questions, or making suggestions about the writing content, go back and reread with the student. Make any changes to the content. Then correct misspellings by circling the incorrect word and writing the correct spelling above the word. Also, correct capitals, periods and other mechanics.

3rd: Before the child leaves you, ask her what she is going to do next as a writer. Will she add to her writing, based on your comments? Will she start publishing her piece?

4th: Thank the child for her efforts and encourage her to keep working hard as a writer!

I hope you enjoy sharing the students' writing! Thanks again for your help!

Sincerely,

CHAPTER 7

Classroom Management and Student Accountability

The key to a workshop that works is engagement. If students are excited about writing, believe in its importance, and are encouraged to write about things they care about while their voices are honored, they will be engaged. When writing time is alive with engagement, management and accountability issues are diminished. Inevitably, though, there are times when all is not running smoothly. In this chapter, you'll find techniques for working through the trouble spots and for heightening student accountability for their writing.

Stop and Problem-Solve

When management problems occur, I stop the workshop and call students together for a problem-solving session.

I say, "I'm sorry, authors, but I have to interrupt your work. We need to stop and come together to talk about what's going on in writing workshop today."

Once students have gathered, I pose two questions (here's another opportunity for them to use their Think Pads to jot down their thoughts). "Take a few minutes to consider: First, what is going well in the workshop today? Second, what is not going well and what might we do about that?"

After a few minutes, we share. Then we generate solutions for the problems. For each proposed solution, I ask, "How might that work out?" so students thoroughly think things through. Of course, this method puts the responsibility for improving the workshop squarely on the students, where it belongs. We come up with a plan of action and implement it. If our plan doesn't work, I stop the workshop for the day—no more Open Writing Time, no conferences, no sharing. Students are devastated if this happens, but it sends a message: "Our writing time is precious. Treat it as such."

Stopping the workshop in progress to problem-solve really works. Since students dearly want their Writing Workshop time, they are often skilled at finding solutions. However, this strategy should only be used for serious infractions—when many writers are finding it difficult to work for one reason or another. Obviously, small problems need to be dealt with through conferring with individuals. Constantly interrupting the workshop diminishes the effectiveness of the technique.

Individual Meetings to Set Individual Goals

The idea of individually meeting with students who are experiencing difficulty has come up several times already. That's because it is the main technique I use for handling any kind of problem, whether academic or behavioral. Remember the student who didn't use conventions at grade level? I suggested meeting with her to set the goal of Circling Skills We Know (page 63) in her writing more frequently than was required of others. Remember the student who wrote interesting story beginnings, created elaborate book covers, but didn't do much else? We met, picked a piece, set goals, and saw it through to publication. The key to making this work is to be specific about expectations, break reasonable goals down into small chunks, and delineate clear steps for achieving them. Most important, you must follow through. When students are having trouble, frequent check-ins are essential. Again, be sure to celebrate their small achievements as they work toward bigger goals.

Think of it this way: If the student at issue was struggling in math, how would you handle it? If he was struggling in reading, how would you handle it? The techniques you'd normally use to intervene will work with writing; namely: differentiate instruction and practice, scaffold, give feedback and adjust assignments for success.

Common Question

"What if you have a student who is constantly disrupting the workshop?"

First of all, don't let her get you down. Realize the important nature of your work, look at the big picture, and remember the benefits writing has for *all* your students. Know, too, as with anything else, students aren't going to be 100 percent on task 100 percent of the time. However, when a student is chronically disruptive and setting individual goals hasn't improved the situation, I have her bring a clipboard and her writing and follow me around as I conference. I say something like, "Since you're unable to handle yourself appropriately, you'll have to stay close to me so I can quickly redirect you if a problem occurs. When you show signs of being able to manage yourself, we can try giving you more freedom again." I use this as a last resort. Since students don't want the stigma of being glued to the teacher, it often solves the problem.

Weekly Check-In

Student accountability for writing is a big issue. Some teachers feel they adequately hold their students accountable through their daily lessons, circulating, habitual sharing, peer review, and their own conferencing. If, however, you feel you need further checks and balances, try the Weekly Check-in.

Have a group of students turn in their Think Pads and writing folders on their assigned day of the week for your review. I tell students, "As you know, writers, I am always interested in how your writing is coming along. So, one day each week, I will ask you to turn in your writing so I can take a look. I like to see the progress you're making, how our Quick Jots and assignments are going, and what current interests are driving your writing during workshop. Sometimes, I may decide we need to conference together. At other times, I may ask you to share something with the class for our next mini-lesson. These quick checks are important, since we are all accountable for how we use our writing time. At the end of the day today, I'll ask Team One to turn in their Think Pads and folders. I will hand them back at the beginning of class tomorrow. At the end of the day tomorrow, Team Two will turn in their writing, and so on."

After school, I briefly look through each child's writing. I do not edit anything, or, usually, read any single piece in its entirety. But this quick review gives me a good handle on all of my writers. It helps me determine which mini-lessons need to be taught or revisited. Additionally, by regularly collecting students' writing, I'm once again communicating my intense interest in their work, and they are reminded of their own accountability.

Follow-Up

Some teachers make a quick notation in their grade books about students' performance as part of their Weekly Check-in. Given the way my district's recording system and report cards are set up, I use a four-point rubric to mark our writing standards. For example, one of our standards is for students to spell grade-level, high-frequency words correctly. I can look for this during my quick check and assign students a 4 if they routinely spell these words correctly ("mastering"), a 3 if they mostly spell them correctly ("developing"), a 2 if they only sometimes spell them correctly ("beginning"), and a 1 if they don't spell these words correctly ("not yet").

Another way to quickly determine level of proficiency is to look at it this way, if a student has "mastered" something, his writing (or other work, for that matter) should appear to need very little or no intervention or support from you in the particular area you are evaluating. He has it down almost all of the time. If a student is "developing" a skill or strategy, his writing could use some intervention or support from you in the focus area. "Beginning" in a standard means the work could use substantial intervention or support. A student gets a 1 if his work could use so much intervention or support, it would likely require intensive effort and time ("not yet"). (This is especially true for skill-based standards like "spells grade-level words correctly.") You might use this four-point system to focus on one indicator a week, if desired. This technique is efficient and can yield a lot of useful data. But, keep in mind, this is only one way to collect data. You can certainly take anecdotal records during Weekly Check-ins or not collect any data at all.

Try It!

Use the four-point scale to quickly score the following two fifth-grade writing samples about family for effective use of voice.

Sample 1:	**Sample 2:**
My family has four members. They are my mom, my dad, my sister and me. We like doing things together like camping and hiking. We really love the outdoors. My sister is two years older than me. She is very good at fishing. She always seems to catch all the fish. My mom fries the fish for our family. We love to eat the fish we catch. One summer we ate fish every week.	Here's a little ditty about my sister. Her name is Aurora. Her name fits her since she is a roaring four year old! She makes me crazy sometimes with her yelling. She only knows how to be loud. "Aaarrrggghhh!" But, can you blame her? It's hard to get attention sometimes in our family of eight. She has red, red hair and she brags about it. Don't try to brush it 'cause she'll scream! In case you didn't guess, her hair fits her, too. It can be fun to play with her, especially when she is in a good mood. So, she has her positive points. I guess, when it's all said and done, she is a good kid.

How long did that take you? It can and should be kept simple. However, when you encounter samples with less stark contrast, still challenge yourself to be efficient and quick. After all, if you do Check-ins regularly, you'll be on top of student growth and can adjust your conclusions accordingly. Hint: When evaluating a standard, it helps to pick a top and bottom sample to serve as anchors like the figures above, and go from there.

Another helpful thing to do is to keep benchmark examples at levels 4, 3, 2 and 1 (just one sample per standard or indicator should do), so you have something concrete to show parents and to assist your own decision making from year to year. I keep mine in a notebook with tabs. I started the notebook by simply pulling one sample for each level the very first time I evaluated for a standard. I made a mental note to keep doing this as I worked through the year looking at different standards over time. The following year, I changed a few samples because I felt I'd come across stronger examples. This proved to be a nice, calm way to produce a truly useful resource I continue to rely on!

By the way, I scored the first fifth-grade sample as a 1 and the second as a 4. Sure, one could argue up or down. But, what's the point of that? I'm keeping data to help me improve instruction—not to wear down writers. If I was to find, for example, several students whose writing voice fell in the 1 and 2 categories, I'd know I need to focus more concretely on building voice during my whole-class mini-lessons.

Variations

Perhaps a Weekly Check-in seems excessive with all you already know about your writers. If this is the case, try this quick teacher review biweekly or tri-weekly. On the flip side, if you have struggling students, even more frequent checks are advisable, as we've discussed throughout this volume.

Common Question

"If we don't have students revise, edit, and formally rewrite most everything they write, do they still take their work seriously?"

Yes, as I mentioned previously, I emphasize the spirit of doing our best in all the writing we do. If you know how to spell it, spell it. If you know how to punctuate it correctly, punctuate it correctly. The part that's often missing is that students don't practice these skills enough in context to become automatic with them, allowing them to be applied almost unconsciously. Again, that's where Circling Skills We Know and all the periodic checks and reviews come in.

Lastly, as I'm sure you've already garnered, an important part of accountability is the overall tone of the classroom. My expectations are high, the pace of instruction is brisk, there's a serious spirit, and students are respectful of one another and the writing process. This goes a long way toward ensuring that students "toe the line" in their writing.

CONCLUSION

My closing thoughts turn to my aspirations for this book . . . and its limitations. The possibility of motivating more writing in classrooms is so exciting! How different education could be if more teachers came to understand the power of writing and provided ongoing opportunities for students—treating the subject much like reading. I hope I've supplied enough food for thought and action here! Yet, there is more to be said about assessment, evaluation, writing nonfiction, working with strugglers, and so on. That's where the voices of others come in. The masters I've referenced, along with several others, have all kinds of ideas and inspiration to offer through their words. After rereading chapters from their books, I return to class with renewed enthusiasm for the magic of writing. The idea behind this volume is to give you enough to get started with success, then you can always delve deeper into your study of writing. But don't underestimate your own power. Jump in with both feet and problem-solve as you go. Believe in yourself, believe in your students, and believe in the process. Give yourself time to make mistakes and grow. Give your students time to make mistakes and grow. Congratulate one another on your accomplishments and take time to notice the wonders writing brings to your lives.

One of my favorite quotes to share with students is "Never miss a day in your writing life!" I have this quote hanging in our classroom and discuss it often. We talk about the joys and discoveries we make through writing. We think of what a shame it would be not to have opportunities to write every day. My dream for students is that they will be lifelong writers who want to write—who need to write.

Years ago, I had a struggling second-grade student, Zach, who was identified as a selective mute. He didn't talk much at school to anyone, had difficulty reading and writing, and went to speech

Hi Mom
Welcome to the Wag's Flag's! My team name is Winners! I'm getting ready for 3rd grade. I'm excited about 3rd grade. I've never lost a writing day in my live.
Love
Zach

therapy for articulation, production, and general language issues. He began the year writing only in partial phrases.

Like everyone else, Zach was accepted into our writing community with open arms. After several weeks, he would sometimes whisper parts of his pieces to me and I responded energetically with specific comments about what he had written. Zach could tell I was listening.

After several months, Zach began taking us up on informal opportunities to share and Author's Chair. He'd sit in the chair and whisper as he read. The other writers were great about it, so silent and attentive. They knew this was a monumental step.

You can tell where this story is going. Zach made amazing progress that year as a writer, reader, thinker, and speaker. Imagine how thrilled I was when I read the letter he wrote to his mother before our last parent-teacher-student conference (shown on previous page). It reminds me of the difference we can make every day in the writing lives of children.

REFERENCES

PROFESSIONAL RESOURCES:

Bureau of Education and Research (BER). Staff Development Video Training Programs: *Enhancing students' growth as writers, Part I and II.*

Bureau of Education and Research (BER). Staff Development Video Training Program: *Using six trait mini-lessons to strengthen your students' writing.*

Calkins, L. M. (1991). *Living between the lines.* Portsmouth, NH: Heinemann.

Calkins, L. M. (1994). *The art of teaching writing.* Portsmouth, NH: Heinemann.

Cazden, C. B. (1991). Contemporary issues and future directions: Active learners and active teachers. In J. Flood, J. M. Jensen, D. Lapp, and J. R. Squire (Eds.), *Handbook of research on teaching the English language arts* (pp. 418–422). New York: Guilford.

Cunningham, P. M. (1995). *Phonics they use: Words for reading and writing.* New York: HarperCollins.

Culham, R. (2003). *6 + 1 traits of writing: The complete guide (grades 3 and up).* New York: Scholastic.

Culham, R. (2005). *6 + 1 traits of writing: The complete guide for the primary grades.* New York: Scholastic.

Elbow, P. (1973). *Writing without teachers.* New York: Oxford University Press.

Fletcher, R. & Portalupi, J. (2001). *Writing workshop: The essential guide.* Portsmouth, NH: Heinemann.

Knapp, M. S. (1995). *Teaching for meaning in high-poverty classrooms.* New York: Teachers College Press.

Murphy, D. Using Six Trait mini-lessons to strengthen your students' writing, grades 3–6. [training video] Bellevue, WA: Bureau of Education and Research.

Murray, W. (1995). A talk with Donald Graves. *Instructor, 105*(4), 42–43.

National Commission on Writing in America's Schools and Colleges. *"The neglected 'R': The need for a writing revolution."* College Entrance Examination Board: 2003.

Raphael, T. E., Highfield, K., & Au, K. H. (2006). *QAR now: A powerful and practical framework that develops comprehension and higher-level thinking in all students.* New York: Scholastic.

Sitton, R. (1999). *Increasing student spelling achievement.* Scottsdale, AZ: Egger Publishing, Inc.

Templeton, S. (2003). "Spelling." in Flood, J., Lapp, D., Squire, J. R., & Jensen, J. M. (Eds.), *Handbook of Research on Teaching the English Language Arts* (2nd ed., pp. 738–751). Mahwah, NY: Lawrence Erlbaum Associates.

Wagstaff, J. M. (1994). *Phonics that work! New strategies for the reading/writing classroom.* New York: Scholastic.

Wagstaff, J. M. (1997). Building practical knowledge of letter-sound correspondences: A beginner's word wall and beyond. *The reading teacher, 51*(4), 298–304.

Wagstaff, J. M. (1999). *Teaching reading and writing with word walls.* New York: Scholastic.

Wagstaff, J. M. (2003). *20 weekly word study poetry packets.* New York: Scholastic.

Wagstaff, J. M. (2009). *Using name walls to teach reading and writing.* New York: Scholastic.

CHILDREN'S BOOKS:

Gardiner, J. R. (1992). *Stone fox.* New York: HarperCollins.

George, K. O. (1999). *Little dog poems.* New York: Clarion.

Park, B. (1998). *Junie B. Jones is a beauty shop guy.* New York: Random House.

Paulus, T. (1972). *Hope for the flowers.* Mahwah, NJ: Paulist Press.

Pilkey, D. (1996). When cats dream. New York, Orchard.

Reynolds, P. (2003). *The dot.* Somerville, MA: Candlewick Press.

Reynolds, P. (2004). *Ish.* Somerville, MA: Candlewick Press.

Viorst, J. (1971). *The tenth good thing about Barney.* New York: Atheneum.